Haiti since 1804

Haiti since 1804

Critical Perspectives on Class, Power, and Gender

ALEX DUPUY

ROWMAN & LITTLEFIELD
Lanham • Boulder • New York • London

Published by Rowman & Littlefield
An imprint of The Rowman & Littlefield Publishing Group, Inc.
4501 Forbes Boulevard, Suite 200, Lanham, Maryland 20706
www.rowman.com

86-90 Paul Street, London EC2A 4NE

Copyright © 2024 by The Rowman & Littlefield Publishing Group, Inc.

All rights reserved. No part of this book may be reproduced in any form or by any electronic or mechanical means, including information storage and retrieval systems, without written permission from the publisher, except by a reviewer who may quote passages in a review.

British Library Cataloguing in Publication Information Available

Library of Congress Cataloging-in-Publication Data Available

ISBN: 978-1-5381-8825-5 (cloth)
ISBN: 978-1-5381-8826-2 (pbk.)
ISBN: 978-1-5381-8827-9 (electronic)

Contents

Acknowledgments   vii

Introduction   1

1. Indemnity, Debt, and Development: A Reprise   5
2. The US Occupation, Foreign Capital, and Transformation of the Haitian Economy   41
3. The Political Economy of Class and Gender in Haiti   61
4. Whither Haiti after Moïse?   89

Bibliography   113

Index   151

About the Author   161

Acknowledgments

I wish to express my gratitude to my wife, Wanda, for her unwavering support while I worked on this project over the past few years.

I want to thank Robert Fatton Jr., for his comments and suggestions on several chapters, and Linden Lewis, Carolyn Fick, Carolle Charles, and Barry Truchil for theirs on different chapters.

I also thank my editor, Michael Tan, who offered helpful editorial suggestions at every stage of this project.

Introduction

This book deals with the theme of class, power, and gender and their interrelations and effects in Haiti in the context of its position and function in the capitalist world economy since 1804.

Chapter One, "Indemnity, Debt, and Development: A Reprise," is a revised version of the chapter "Property, Debt, and Development: Rethinking the Indemnity Question," originally published in *Rethinking the Haitian Revolution: Slavery, Independence, and the Struggle for Recognition* (2019). The prevailing view among historians is that in 1825 Haitian president Jean-Pierre Boyer, fearing a war with France, capitulated to its demand of an indemnity of 150 million francs to compensate the former colonial property owners in return for its recognition of Haiti's independence. Most analysts also attribute Haiti's inability to develop its economy during the nineteenth century to what *The New York Times* referred to as the "ransom" that Haiti was forced to pay to its former colonial master.

I offer a different argument that focuses instead on the agency of Haiti's postindependence rulers who saw the recognition of Haiti's independence as the sine qua non of its postindependence development. President Alexandre Pétion first raised the idea of such a quid pro quo to France in 1812, and President Boyer, who succeeded Pétion in 1818, concluded an agreement with France in 1825. They did so, I show, to secure the transfer of property rights from the former colonial proprietors to Haitians. Moreover, the burden of the indemnity that was paid off in full in 1883 was not the principal reason Haiti could not develop its economy in the nineteenth century. It was due instead to the inability of the new dominant classes to expropriate and proletarianize the land-owning/-possessing farmers to recreate the plantation system of the colonial era, on the one hand, and the internecine conflicts among political factions to control the state as a means of enrichment, on the other.

Chapter Two, "The US Occupation, Foreign Capital, and Transformation of the Haitian Economy," has three objectives. The first is to show how the occupation of Haiti by the United States from 1915 to 1934 was part of its objective to substitute its political and economic dominance in the hemisphere for that of its European rivals, France especially in the case of Haiti. The second focuses on the proletarianization of Haitian farmers and peasants, the investment of US and Canadian capital in agricultural and industrial production, and the export of Haitian workers to work on US-owned plantations in other countries in the Caribbean and Central America. And the third analyzes the conflicts between the mulatto and black factions of the dominant classes to control the state that led to the 29-year dictatorship of François Duvalier and that of his son Jean-Claude from 1957 to 1986, and whose ouster and exile paved the way for the election of the former priest and proponent of Liberation Theology Jean-Bertrand Aristide in 1990. Overthrown in February 1991, reelected in 2001, and overthrown again in 2004, Aristide caved to the neoliberal policies imposed by the United States and the international financial institutions (International Monetary Fund, World Bank, and Agency for International Development). Consequently, Haiti became the supplier of the lowest-paid labor for the export assembly and the largest importer of foods from the United States in the Caribbean, especially rice.

Chapter Three, "The Political Economy of Class and Gender in Haiti," offers a critique of the argument developed by Mireille Neptune Anglade in her seminal book *L'autre moitié du développement: à propos du travail des femmes en Haïti* (1986), that in Haiti women in general labor for the benefit and the enrichment of men in general. Alternatively, I argue that the men and women of the dominant classes exploit and are enriched by the labor of men and women in the subordinate classes, notwithstanding the discriminations women face in the workplace and society at large. By contrast, women who live off the land (as landowners or tenant farmers), or as market vendors, exercise a greater degree of autonomy and are often the primary earners of income for their family. Changing the unequal gender relations that characterize Haitian society, then, requires transforming its unequal gender and class relations, and creating a state that prioritizes the interests of the majority. The chapter draws on propositions offered by women's organizations to achieve those ends.

Chapter Four, "Whither Haiti after Moïse?" focuses on two separate but related dynamics that are having a significant impact on all aspects of Haitian society. The first is the political crisis that has paralyzed Haiti since the assassination of President Jovenel Moïse on July 7, 2021. With a poorly trained and equipped police force, violent and criminal gangs vying for power now control most of the capital city of Port-au-Prince and other parts of the country by killing and/or kidnaping thousands of citizens for ransom and driving them from their homes. De facto Prime Minister Ariel Henry has called on foreign powers to intervene and is considering mobilizing the Haitian army that was disbanded in 1995 to confront and suppress the gangs. That has not happened. Grassroots organizations oppose a foreign military intervention and are calling instead for support to help the Haitian police to combat the gangs and create the conditions for elections and a new democratic order that will prioritize and serve the interests of the majority.

Second, the crisis gripping the country, combined with the economic transformations described above, spurred more emigration, which has become a mainstay for increasing numbers of families and the economy that now rely on the remittances from emigrants that account for more than a quarter of its gross domestic product.

1

Indemnity, Debt, and Development: A Reprise[1]

Every student of Haitian history knows that in July 1825 Haitian president Jean-Pierre Boyer accepted the ordinance of King Charles X of France, which stipulated the following conditions for the recognition of Haiti's independence:

> 1) The ports of the French part of Saint-Domingue will remain open to all nations. The duties collected at these ports, whether on the ships or on goods, whether incoming or outgoing, will be the same for those under the flags of all nations except for those under the flag of France and for which they will be reduced by half. 2) The inhabitants of the French part of Saint-Domingue will pay to France, in five equal installments the sum of 150 million francs intended to compensate the former colonial proprietors who demand to be indemnified. And 3) We concede, by the present Ordinance and under those conditions, to the actual inhabitants of the French part of Saint-Domingue, the full and complete independence of their government. (AP-1-20 *Ordonnance du Roi*, 17 Avril 1825)

The sum of 150 million francs was based on the revenues of the colonial properties (sugar, coffee, cotton, indigo) in 1789 (Coradin 1988, 202–203; Blancpain 2001, 56–57; Buffaerts 2021, 105). As Buffaerts (2021) points out, the a posteriori justification of the 150 million francs responded to several objectives: It allowed King Charles X to bypass the French Revolution and return to 1789, and it favored the colonial property owners insofar as their creditors could only claim 10 percent of their debts (107).

It is also well known that in a second treaty with France in 1838 Boyer succeeded in reducing the total amount to be paid to France to 60 million francs with annual installments spread over 30 years; lowering the interest rate on the 30 million francs Haiti borrowed from a French bank to make the initial payment on the original 150 million francs indemnity from 6 to 3 percent; and eliminating the half duties Haiti had to pay on its exports to France, but which it had already stopped paying before the treaty. Haiti paid off the indemnity in full in 1883, that is, in 58 years (45 if one bases it on the 1838 treaty) instead of 30 (MAE-CP v. 8, *Ordonnance du Roi*, 30 May 1838; Blancpain 2001, 63–74).

Historians generally agree on the following sequence that led to the final acceptance of the ordinance, much of it based on the report of baron de Mackau to the Comte de Chabrol, as well as on the Mémoires of Joseph Baltazar Inginac (1843), Boyer's secretary-general. Mackau arrived in Port-au-Prince on July 4, 1825, with a flotilla of 14 French war ships stationed off the bay of Port-au-Prince. He met with Boyer's emissaries Inginac, Senator Rouanez, and Colonel Frémont. They raised objections to the first clause of the ordinance, which they interpreted as maintaining France's sovereignty over Haiti and giving it the right to intervene in its internal affairs. According to them, that clause contradicted the third clause that recognized Haiti's independence. The emissaries then briefed Boyer who agreed with their reasons for rejecting the ordinance, but he decided to meet with Mackau alone. The first day of their meeting ended inconclusively. Boyer believed the 150 million francs indemnity was far above what he (and President Alexandre Pétion before him) had considered "reasonable" and beyond Haiti's means, and that the tariff reductions France demanded were excessive and needed to be reduced. Nonetheless, he subsequently accepted those terms because, as he said, he "wanted to be done with it."[2] But he maintained that he could not accept the first clause because it was an affront to Haiti's honor and the rights it had won and would defend. He then proposed to write to Charles X to ask him to clarify that it did not mean what he believed it did, after which he would accept the ordinance and get it ratified by the Senate.

When they met the next day, Mackau handed Boyer a note he had prepared in which he made clear that based on the directives he had received personally from the King before he left for Haiti, he could certify that the first clause did not in any way mean that France intended to maintain some sort of suzerainty over Haiti or the right to interfere in its internal affairs; that the notion of keeping all ports open to the flags of all nations was part of the agreement the independent powers of Europe had reached at the Congress of Verona in 1822; that the King of France was not trying to take away with one hand (i.e., the stipulations of the first clause) what he was granting with the other (i.e., the third clause, which recognized Haiti's full and complete independence); and that he was certain the amount of the indemnity and the tariffs could be renegotiated. But first and foremost, the ordinance had to be accepted and ratified as written.

Mackau then made the following proposition: His orders were strict, and he could not negotiate the terms of the ordinance.[3] But if Boyer accepted the ordinance and had it ratified, he, Mackau, would stay as a hostage in Haiti and would send an emissary to France to get the certification Boyer wanted. Otherwise, he would have to carry out his orders to their full extent, meaning the blockade of Haiti's ports until Haiti accepted the ordinance. This meant, of course, that France and Haiti would be at war. Boyer replied verbally and in writing that this would not be necessary, that he was satisfied with the explanation he was given, and that he would accept the ordinance. He then proceeded with its ratification by the Senate (Madiou 1988, VI: 448–463; Ardouin 1958, 9: 76–78; Inginac 1843, 70–73; Mackau AP-156-1-20, 7 juillet 1825; Boyer AP-1-20, 8 juillet 1825; Léger 1930, 130–136; Brière 2012, 112–114; Coradin 1988, 191–196).

As would be expected, different interpretations of Boyer's decision to accept the ordinance abound. For Beaubrun Ardouin, Boyer had no choice but to accept the ordinance given the international context in which Haiti found itself. Great Britain and the United States, two of Haiti's most important trading nations since 1804, refused to recognize Haiti's independence even though they had done so for the rebellious Spanish colonies in South America. Inginac advised Boyer to accept it for the same reasons (Ardouin 1958, 9: 88–89; Inginac 1843, 71–72). Jean Coradin advanced a similar view. Boyer, he argued, was negotiating under pressure of a possible confrontation with France and knew that he could not count on the English or the United States to support him. The question was whether to risk a war for which he was not prepared or accept the ordinance: "everything seemed to suggest that it was to resolve that dilemma that he accepted the ordinance" (1988, 197).

Thomas Madiou, on the other hand, concluded that Mackau's "clarifications" to Boyer were nothing more than "an ultimatum sugarcoated with delicate and polite terms: it was either accept the ordinance or war." Boyer capitulated, according to him (Madiou 1988, VI: 460). Abel-Nicolas Léger also argued that Boyer sold out: "Haitian diplomacy had capitulated on all points in 1825. Public opinion let Boyer and France know that the Ordinance of April 17 did not accord with its expectations. That moment marked the beginning of the tenacious opposition to Boyer that would culminate 18 years later in the Praslin uprising" against him (1930, 141).[4] Victor Schoelcher advanced a similar view: Boyer "was afraid of the French flotilla, and that is why [Haitian] patriots condemned his pusillanimity and never forgave him for the way he concluded that negotiation" (1843, 167).

Largely based on the same belief that Boyer was forced to pay the indemnity, former Haitian president Jean-Bertrand Aristide demanded that France repay Haiti the equivalent sum of $21,685,135,571.48 for the 90 million francs in a speech he gave on April 7, 2003, to commemorate the bicentenary of Toussaint Louverture's death. The reimbursement combined what Aristide termed restitution for the indemnity and reparation for the enslavement of Africans in Saint-Domingue (Aristide 2003). The French government predictably rejected Aristide's demands outright (Radio Métropole, 9 avril 2003), but appointed a commission led by the well-known writer Régis Debray to issue a report to respond to Aristide. Titled "Haïti et la France: Rapport À Dominique de Villepin ministre des Affaires ètrangères" (2004), it disingenuously claimed that Aristide's demands had no legal standing because the right of nations to self-determination did not exist in 1838 (when France recognized Haiti's independence), and neither did the concept of slavery as a crime against humanity, which was not recognized as such until after World War II. Moreover, the report went on, France had offered substantial bilateral and international foreign aid to Haiti during the past century, but only to have it mismanaged (Debray 2004).

The French government, however, had a more direct way of dealing with Aristide. A year after his demand, France joined the United States and Canada in supporting the organized opposition to Aristide and the rebel soldiers of the former Haitian army who toppled and exiled him, first to the Central African Republic and later to South Africa in 2004, where he remained until he returned to Haiti in 2011 (Dupuy 2014, 112–114; Caroit 2004).

More recently *The New York Times* published a series of reports titled "The Ransom: The Roots of Haiti's Misery: Reparations to Enslavers." Its authors argued that Haiti was "forced to pay the descendants of the former slave masters"; that "the burden continued well into the 20th century" and "hobbled the country for more than 100 years"; and that had the estimated $21 billion Haiti would have had if the money had stayed in the country [as Aristide had claimed], it would have boosted its economic growth. The report concluded that "The loss to Haiti is astounding: about $115 billion over time, or eight times the size of its economy in 2020" (Porter et al. 2022).

FROM TOUSSAINT LOUVERTURE TO JEAN-PIERRE BOYER

The Making of a Landed Bourgeoisie

In contrast to the arguments summarized above that interpreted Boyer's acceptance of the indemnity as a capitulation or as having no choice but to do so, I offer a different view that focuses instead on the class interests Boyer, and Pétion before him, were defending when they offered to pay an indemnity to compensate the former colonial property owners in return for France's recognition of Haiti's independence. To be sure, the international context in which Haiti was operating was fundamental in their considerations since Haiti was heavily dependent on international trade and access to the markets of the advanced countries for its products. And given that neither the United States, England, nor any other major power was willing to recognize Haiti's independence before France did so gave the latter considerable leverage in its negotiations with Haiti. So frustrated was Boyer over France's refusal to recognize Haiti's independence that he asked in a letter he wrote on May 16, 1821, to Esmangart, a former colonist who had been charged with reopening negotiations with Haiti: "The efforts France made on its part to ensure Washington's triumph, did they not bring fame to the regime of Louis XVI? Impressed by these examples, Haitians are asking themselves often why that latter power hesitates to repudiate such vain rights to reap more honorable benefits.... Could the difference in skin color be the reason for this hesitation?" (cited in Madiou 1988, 6: 198–199).

Commenting on that letter, Madiou argued that skin color was not the issue. Rather, he suggested, France regretted relinquishing its once wealthiest colony in the New World and was attempting to "establish a protectorate in the interest of its preponderance in the Antilles and the Gulf of Mexico which centrally overlook the two Americas" (Ibid.). No doubt, France could not come to terms with the loss of its most productive and wealthiest colony in the Americas. But the "race question" in fact could not be so easily separated from France's economic and political interests. As I will point out, just as Bonaparte sent Leclerc to retake possession of Saint-Domingue in 1801 to restore slavery and the racial order of the colonial regime, so did King Louis XVIII in his attempt to reassert France's sovereignty over Haiti. Except for reinstituting a full-scale slave system, his government sought to regain control of its former colony, return the colonial properties to their former owners, and reestablish white supremacy. These objectives were clearly laid out in the instructions that Pierre-Victor Malouet, a former colonist who was now Minister of Marine and the Colonies, gave to the emissaries he sent to Haiti in 1814 to negotiate the terms under which the governments of Alexandre Pétion and Henri Christophe would surrender control of Haiti back to France.

As did Christophe, Pétion and Boyer consistently opposed all attempts by France to reimpose its sovereignty over Haiti before and after the 1825 ordinance even if that meant war. In 1824, after the emissaries he had sent to France failed to reach agreement on a treaty to recognize Haiti's independence in return for an indemnity and reciprocal commercial advantages, Boyer published their report and summarized the history of all the negotiations since 1814:

> In 1814, France sought to impose its complete sovereignty; in 1816, it was a question of a constitutional sovereignty; in 1823 the issue was limited to demanding the indemnity we had offered. Why return to the idea of subjecting us to an external sovereignty in 1824? What is this external sovereignty? From our point of view, it includes two types of rights: one is that of a protectorate; and the other concerns foreign relations, whether political or economic, both of which would then be asserted. But for whom is this sovereignty being thought? However we want to think about this sovereignty, it seems to be injurious or contrary to our security, and that is why we rejected it. (cited in Schoelcher 1843, 164–165)

Schoelcher pointed out that at this point the "French government understood finally that it either had to abandon all relations with the old colony or establish them on mutually recognized and agreed upon grounds. It is on that basis that Charles X [who succeeded Louis XVIII] issued the ordinance of 17 April 1825" (Ibid.; addition mine). If that is the case, then, Boyer accepted the ordinance not because he feared war with France but because he believed it was in his interest and that of the newly emergent Haitian ruling class to do so. For him this was the only way that both the property question that remained at the heart of the conflicts between the former colonial planter class and the Haitian bourgeoisie and the question of independence could be solved simultaneously. By declaring the indemnity a national debt in 1826, Boyer saddled the nation with the bill, which meant that the people would pay the price for servicing the interests of the bourgeoisie (AE/B/III/380, 25 Février 1826; Ardouin 1958, 10: 6). Moreover, Boyer had invaded and occupied the western Spanish colony of Santo Domingo from 1822 to 1844 and taxed its population to help pay off the indemnity (Moya Pons 1972, 29). As Michelle Wucker put it, "Incredible as it was that the Haitian victors had to compensate the losers in their war of independence . . . [u]nder Boyer's plan, Dominican sweat would raise the funds to pay the debt" (1999, 39).

The formation of a new indigenous landed bourgeoisie began with the rise of Toussaint Louverture and his revolutionary army when they gained control of the colony in 1800.[5] That new sector of the dominant class would combine with that of the "free people color," both mulattoes and blacks, who together owned approximately one third of the productive properties—mostly coffee plantations—and one quarter of the slaves before the revolution and the abolition of slavery in 1794 (Moreau de Saint-Méry 1958, 2: 1110, 1138, 1154–1155; 3: 1400; Debien 1950, 214–215). The revolutionary government had committed to maintaining the plantation system and for that to happen it needed to solve two problems simultaneously. The first was that many colonial plantation owners had fled the colony when the revolution broke out, an exodus that continued after Louverture took power in 1800. He encouraged them to return and resume control of their properties. Those who did not or could not because they had fled to a colony of a foreign power at war with France had their properties confiscated by the revolutionary government. Together these properties amounted to two thirds of all the colonial properties under the old regime (Gambart 1802; Cabon 1929, 4: 109).

The revolutionary government then put the confiscated properties under the control of military officers. Many also bought or leased those properties, among them Louverture and Jean-Jacques Dessalines (who would take over the leadership of the revolutionary army after the arrest and deportation of Louverture in 1802). Those officers who had not bought or leased properties but were put in charge of them eventually became their de facto owners. Moreover, if absentee planters returned to reclaim their properties, they were obligated to reimburse the tenants all their expenses to maintain, operate, or improve the properties during the owners' absence. Many of them could not afford to do so and consequently the tenants kept possession of them (Cabon 1929, 4: 193).

The second problem the Louverture government faced was that of labor. Since slavery had been abolished and the former slaves refused to remain on the old plantations and sought instead to gain access to and cultivate their own land, the government took measures to force them to do so. To prevent the breakup of the plantations and parceling them into small farms, the government prohibited the sale of properties smaller than 50 carreaux (1 carreau equals approximately 3 acres). Those who sought to buy land had to prove they did not previously belong to a plantation and that they had the means to do so. They also had to declare what crops they would produce on their land and the number of workers they could employ (Idlinger 1802; Ardouin 1958, 4: 69).

The revolutionary government did not stop at those measures. It issued a draconian decree in 1800 that sought to compel the former slaves who could not prove that they were duly employed or practicing a "useful occupation" to return to their old plantations or face arrest. In return for their labor, the workers would receive one fourth of the net value of the crops produced in addition to being allowed to cultivate their own provision grounds. In effect, then, Louverture militarized the plantations. As Adolphe Cabon put it, under the military officers put in charge of running the plantations that had been abandoned by their former colonial owners, the workers were

> subjected to a servitude that was not the slavery of the old regime, but which must have appeared to them as severe as their old status. The name of slave was abolished, but the military discipline established throughout the country transformed the plantations into a battalion under a chief. . . . [And] the laborer was

constantly constrained to produce more and more, without any aim other than the prosperity of the plantation. (1929, 4: 189)

The postindependence governments of Jean-Jacques Dessalines, Alexandre Pétion, and Henri Christophe failed to deal successfully with either the property or the labor questions. Boyer definitively resolved the first question with the acceptance of the 1825 ordinance, but not the second. On the property side, Toussaint's government and those of his successors were committed to preserving the system of private property ownership of the means of production. Consequently, the problem they confronted was that the expropriation, appropriation, redistribution, and even the sale of colonial properties by these successive governments did not resolve the question of who really owned them insofar as the original titles for those properties remained in the possession of their former colonial owners or their inheritors. That is what the indemnity was meant to solve and did.

The defeat of the French forces at the end of 1803 led the victorious revolutionary army under Dessalines's leadership to declare the colony's independence and rename it Haiti on January 1, 1804. The war of independence, which lasted from August 1802 to December 1803, had been devastating in human and material terms. Claude and Marcel Auguste estimated that a total of approximately 150,000 people had been killed on both sides, and between 100,000 to 130,000 Haitians and 50,000 to 55,000 French had been permanently disabled. The cities of Le Cap, Port-de-Paix, Gonaives, and Saint-Marc had been burned to the ground, and throughout the country plantations, sugar mills, irrigation networks, wharfs, and other businesses had been destroyed, amounting to an estimated value of 1,144,258,948 francs. In essence, this meant that Haiti started off with a ruined economy and infrastructure (Auguste and Auguste 1985, 313–319; Dupuy 1989, 74).

Once in control of the state, Dessalines moved swiftly to consolidate his power by imposing a military dictatorship throughout the country and expulsing or killing the French who remained. French forces still occupied parts of Spanish San Domingo and were contemplating a new invasion of Haiti. Dessalines invaded that colony to crush them but returned soon after to prepare for another anticipated French attack that never materialized. In February 1804 Dessalines ordered the arrest, trial, and execution of all the French who had been found guilty of participating or assisting in the murder of Haitians during the last two years under the control of Generals Leclerc and Rochambeau (Ardouin 1958, 6: 14–17; Léger 1930, 12–14; Placide 1826, 425–426; Etienne 1982, 17; Laurent n.d., 94–99).

The government then proceeded to confiscate all the properties that belonged to the French colonialists and declared them national properties, making this the most extensive nationalization of properties in the New World at the time (Mathon 1985, 34). As under Louverture, the new government leased the nationalized properties to functionaries and military officers who, as before, eventually acquired them. At the same time, laborers who had taken over abandoned properties and had no titles to prove ownership of those lands were swiftly dispossessed. Those who did not own land were also prohibited from cutting and selling logwood from public lands. Only military and government functionaries could own and operate the mills on the properties allocated to them.

As Louverture did before him, Dessalines compelled landless or otherwise unemployed laborers to return to their former plantations under military control. He took other steps to promote the rise of a black landed bourgeoisie by dispossessing mulattoes of lands sold or transferred to them after October 1802, primarily in the South where they were dominant. And the 1805 Constitution barred all foreigners (meaning whites of any nationality) from owning real estate property in Haiti. Dessalines's discriminative, corrupt,[6] and repressive regime antagonized not only mulattoes but various sectors of the population, including factions of the military and especially laborers and the landless. Henri Christophe, who was general in chief of the army, contemplated Dessalines's overthrow and even worked secretly with his archrival Alexandre Pétion to do so. An uprising erupted against Dessalines on October 8, 1806, quickly spread to different parts of the country with the support of sectors of the military, and ended with his assassination that same month (Ardouin 1958, 6: 14, 33, 46–50; Placide 1826, 434; Laurent n.d., 128; Saint-Rémy 1956, 10: 40, 45–47; Léger, 1907, 158; Dupuy 1989, 77–80).

No sooner was Dessalines gone that a conflict erupted between the factions of the dominant classes allied with Christophe, on the one hand, and Pétion, on the other, that led to the partition of the country into two states. Christophe, who gained control of the North province and renamed it the State of Haiti, had himself proclaimed king. He rallied behind him those who had risen to positions of power under Louverture's and Dessalines's respective governments and were predominantly black. For his part, Pétion took control of the West and the South,[7] and had the support of the predominantly mulatto bourgeoisie whose origins dated back to the colonial period before the rise of Toussaint Louverture. Neither Christophe nor Pétion pursued a "politics of color" sensu stricto because each appointed mulattoes and blacks to top positions in their respective administrations. But blacks benefited most under Christophe as did mulattoes under Pétion.

Christophe also attempted to revitalize the plantation system by compelling landless workers to live and work on the farms where they were assigned or hired. Those workers could leave the plantations only with the authorization of their owners or managers. They, as under Louverture, were to receive one fourth of the value of the products and were allocated provision grounds, and he also resorted to forced or corvée labor. Christophe established commercial relations with Great Britain to weaken France's influence and tried in vain to gain England's recognition of Haiti's independence. He gave foreigners who brought their businesses to his kingdom guarantees to protect their properties (Code Henry, esp. "Loi Concernant la Culture"; Leyburn 1941, 45; Moral 1961, 31; Moore 1972, 25; Cole 1967, 209–210; Nicholls 1979, 52–53; Franklin 1828/1970, 201; Clarkson 1952, 47, 108–109, 268–271).

By contrast, Pétion, confronted with a peasant rebellion in parts of the southwest in 1807 that lasted until he died in 1818 and was not fully crushed until 1819 by his successor, Jean-Pierre Boyer, pursued a more liberal land and labor policy than Christophe did in the north and used his agrarian policy as a weapon in his conflicts with the latter. In addition to returning the lands Dessalines had taken from mulatto property owners to them, he preserved the lands that had been placed under the national domain. As his predecessors had done, he leased or sold public lands to high-ranking military officers and public officials. But he also made land grants to lower-ranking officers and mid-level civil servants, as well as to rural laborers. Nonetheless, the wealthiest landowners appropriated the best and largest properties and benefited from tax exemptions on coffee and sugar production. Pétion himself took over the Ferron de la Ferronnays sugar plantation in the Cul de Sac (one of the most productive regions in the colony) and passed it on to Boyer after his death in 1818, who already owned several other properties in different parts of the country (Cheney 2017, 211; Moral 1961, 40).

As with the previous regimes, laborers were still paid one fourth the value of the crops, and they were also granted their own provision plots. But the plantations were not militarized, and workers could leave them with special permits to go beyond their parish. Vagrants were more harshly punished. In short, it could be argued that because of the more "liberal" nature of Pétion's regime, the repression of workers had to be opaque and shrouded in a greater appearance of liberality (Leyburn 1941; Manigat 1962; Moral 1961; Nicholls 1979; Pierre-Charles 1967; Péan 2000).

Rising to power in 1818 as president of the Republic of Haiti after Pétion's death, and of a reunified country in 1820 after Christophe's, Boyer reverted to the draconian land and labor policies of Louverture, Dessalines, and Christophe embodied in his 1826 Code Rural. As those of his predecessors, Boyer's Code declared that workers had an obligation to labor on and were bound to the plantations to which they were assigned. Workers could not form cooperatives but had to sign contracts with the landowners and receive one fourth to one half of the gross revenues, or in some cases be paid in wages (Boyer 1992). Notwithstanding these draconian policies, Boyer was not able to reconstitute the large-scale plantations of old, largely because to do so would have required the expropriation of the medium and small farmers who had benefited from Pétion's more liberal redistributive policies and suppress the rural population who had gained access to state-owned properties and produced crops for both the domestic and export markets and their own consumption.

Boyer also imposed the Code Rural in Santo Domingo and met with opposition there as well. Largely due to the different system of property ownership and distribution in Santo Domingo, Dominican landowners challenged the government and were supported by Dominican merchants when Boyer sought to close several ports open to foreign trade. As Moya Pons put it, "Boyer failed to integrate both parts of the island, not only because Dominicans were opposed to his agrarian policies but also because his own countrymen were opposed to them" (1998, 139).

By the time of the "Praslin Revolution" of 1843, which led to Boyer's overthrow and exile in March of that year, a significant opposition to him led by the more liberal wing of the Haitian bourgeoisie had coalesced around a series of grievances that demanded an end to the government's authoritarian tendencies and repressive measures, greater freedom of the press and public debate, educational reforms, legislative reforms, and a coherent program of economic development and agricultural reform. It is worth noting, however, that the indemnity Boyer agreed to pay to France was not included in the list of grievances (Leyburn 1941, 66–70; Franklin 1828/1970; Moral 1961, 41–43; Coradin 1988, 295–298; Bellegarde 1938, 110–112).

A QUESTION OF PROPERTY

After Bonaparte's defeat in Saint-Domingue, he turned his gaze on conquering Europe. But that did not work out for him there either. His defeat at Leipzig in 1814 by the quadruple alliance of Austria, England, Prussia, and Russia led to the Paris Treaty of May 1814 and the restoration of King Louis XVIII and the Bourbon dynasty in France. A subsequent treaty in November 1815 reduced the size of France to its 1792 configuration, imposed an indemnity of 700 million francs to be paid to the allied powers in five years, and prohibited it from engaging in armed hostilities against other nations. But it allowed France to keep possession of the Caribbean colonies it still had in 1789, including Saint-Domingue, notwithstanding the fact that it was no longer a colony. The treaty went even further by granting France permission to continue the slave trade for five years and use "whatever means it chose, including armed force, to reappropriate Saint-Domingue and bring it and the population of that colony under its obeisance." The article also stipulated that Britain "reserves the right of its subjects to engage in commercial transactions in the ports of Saint-Domingue that would neither be attacked nor occupied by French authorities" (CC9A-216MIOM-34, 24 juin 1814; France Traité, 20 Novembre 1815; Coradin 1988, 64).

The former colonial planters were also pressing Louis XVIII to recolonize Haiti so they could regain possession of their properties and reestablish the old slave order, an objective that was supported by Pierre-Victor Malouet, the new French Minister of Marine (Clarkson 1952, 57). France knew, however, that having won its independence through a revolution, Haiti would not allow itself to be recolonized peacefully. Since Haiti won its independence England and the United States became its main trading partners, and French ships could come to Haiti only under a foreign flag. Neither of these powers, nor any other Western power, was willing to recognize Haiti's independence until France did so. For the United States in particular, doing so would have meant legitimizing a slave revolution, thereby undermining its own slave regime and its concomitant ideology of white supremacy. But the United States went further by pressuring the other newly independent states of Latin America, including anticolonial revolutionaries like Simon Bolivar to whom Pétion had offered material and military support in his struggle for independence, not to recognize Haiti's independence and exclude it from participating at the Panama Congress of 1826 (Coradin 1988, 141–144; Dupuy 2014, 57). The solidarity among the imperialist powers, therefore, weighed heavily on the new republic and would be highly significant in Boyer's decision to accept the 1825 ordinance.

It is in the context outlined above that one can best understand France's strategy to reassert its dominance, both political and economic, over Haiti. Seeking to exploit the divisions between Christophe and Pétion, the French government dispatched three emissaries, Dauxion-Lavaisse, Franco de Medina, and Draverman to Haiti in July 1814. They were to deal, respectively, with Pétion, Christophe, and Borgella. As I noted in footnote 6, however, the latter had submitted to Pétion in 1812 and no longer controlled any territory, a fact that France obviously did not know (Wallez 1826, 12–13). This meant, then, that the emissaries would be dealing with Christophe and Pétion. Malouet gave the emissaries specific instructions to try to persuade all three (sic) leaders to submit peacefully, but they were also to inform them that if they were uncooperative France was ready to use force.

France's objectives were unambiguous. Seeking to exploit the color divisions and the rivalries between the two factions of the dominant class, the instructions outlined seven key strategies: 1) Mulattoes whose complexions were proximate to those of whites would be fully assimilated and granted more privileges like those accorded to whites. 2) The rest of the mulatto caste would be granted political rights but with some exceptions that would keep them subordinate to whites. 3) All others whose complexions are less proximate to whites would have lesser rights. 4) All free blacks would have less advantages. 5) All blacks who are currently working on plantations, and those who freed themselves from those obligations, would be reassigned to their old plantations. 6) The number of blacks who would be freed would be limited. And 7) Those who could not be freed but were considered too dangerous would be expelled from the colony.

Once these conditions had been met and agreed upon by the current rulers, the following conditions would be added: 1) Property rights and all those that guarantee them must be reestablished and respected, such that all those former colonial owners who had titles, inherited them, or had notary certificates of ownership, would regain possession of their properties. And 2) All peoples of color would have political rights and the property owners among them would be assimilated if it was understood that such rights and those who would fulfill higher or lower positions in the civil administration and the military were not acquired rights but were granted at the discretion of the King. Those who oversaw the colonial government would submit to the authority of the King, and they would assure those members of their castes who obeyed them of the good graces of the King, but without imposing any obligations or demands on his authority. Once these conditions were met and the current heads of the colonial government certified their submission in writing, they would be freed of all future responsibilities ("Instructions," in Wallez 1826, 186–189).

Christophe and Pétion responded differently to these revelations. As I mentioned previously, Christophe disdained the French, favored closer ties with England, and was seeking its recognition of Haiti's independence. When Medina crossed into Christophe's domain from Santo Domingo, Christophe had him captured and brought to Cap Haïtien. Malouet's instructions were found on him. He was interrogated, jailed, and executed.[8] Christophe then published all the documents Medina was carrying, and sent them, including Medina's interrogation, to Pétion. He in turn sent them to Dauxion-Lavaisse who acknowledged their authenticity. With the real intentions of France exposed, Pétion asked Dauxion-Lavaisse to leave Haiti (Ibid., 13–17).

During his monthlong stay in Haiti Dauxion-Lavaisse and Pétion exchanged many letters in which Pétion made it clear that Haiti would never accept any form of French suzerainty and demanded nothing less than France's recognition of Haiti's independence. But in his last letter to Dauxion-Lavaisse of November 27, 1814, Pétion offered what seemed to be an unsolicited quid pro quo: that in "recognizing the rights and independence of Haitians," Haiti would in turn "reconcile with what it owes to certain of the King's subjects[9] . . . [and] work to establish the grounds for an agreed upon indemnity that we will agree to pay" ("Pétion to Dauxion-Lavaisse," in Wallez 1826, 166–170; also cited in Ardouin 1958, 8: 23). As Inginac—who served under both Pétion and Boyer—noted in his Mémoires, Pétion made the offer of an indemnity "for the properties of the old colonists who were henceforth barred from the country, so that the free and independent Republic could deal with France as one nation to another, otherwise war between the two countries would be interminable" (1843, 29).

In early October 1816, the French launched new initiatives to attempt to regain control of Haiti. In a series of exchanges between the French emissaries Esmangart and François Fontanges and Pétion, they tried to convince him to accept French sovereignty over Haiti—which they referred to as "this colony"—by arguing that a country can consider itself independent only if it can defend itself from external threats without having to rely or depend on the support of another power. Given that Haiti did not have the means to do so they considered its independence to be a mere "pipe dream and a pretention it could not sustain." Pétion replied that Haiti would never compromise its independence and accept French rule, even if this meant war and the destruction of its society and economy. He broke off negotiations with the French envoys (FCO Haiti and President Pétion 1816, No. 14, 38–39). For his part, Christophe, who had been reassured by Thomas Clarkson that France was not able to launch a military invasion and that any such consideration "would be considered to be mad ... and as hopeless and disastrous as the Expedition of Leclerc," simply refused to meet with the French envoy (Clarkson 1952, 200; Blancpain 2001, 48–49).

Boyer became president of the Republic after Pétion died in 1818, and the entire country in 1820 after Christophe's suicide. He pursued Pétion's principle of rejecting any form of suzerainty over Haiti but was also willing to offer to pay an indemnity to France in return for its recognition of Haiti's independence. And, as Pétion had done, Boyer twice broke off negotiations with France before 1825—in 1821 with the French envoy Dupetit-Thouars, and in 1824 with the then French Minister of Marine and the Colonies, Clermont-Tonnere—because it continued to insist on subjecting Haiti to its sovereignty. Boyer made that point in an address to the nation on October 18, 1824. In announcing that he had ended negotiations with France, Boyer explained that although he reiterated Pétion's offer to pay a "reasonable" indemnity to France, he had also made it clear that Haiti would accept nothing less than "the full and complete recognition of its independence free of any and all foreign domination, suzerainty, or protectorate by any foreign power." Haitians, he went on to say, would "never deviate from their resolve, and if ever they had to repulse an unjust aggression once again ... they would [vigorously] defend the independence [they had won] and enjoyed for the past twenty years" (*Pièces officielles* 1824).

But France, as I pointed out above, was no longer contemplating or capable of launching another Napoleonesque military expedition despite the clamor among the former colonial property owners and their spokesmen in the French parliament to do so (Dorigny 2021, 24). As Madiou pointed out, once France had learned that the country had been reunited under the leadership of Boyer in 1820, the question of how to deal with Haiti resurfaced. The chambers of commerce of the maritime ports of France recommended to the Duc de Richelieu that France recognize Haiti's independence so that they could establish normal trade relations. Esmangart also advised Louis XVIII to do the same but in return for an indemnity for the colonial property owners, which Pétion had already proposed. In February 1821 Louis XVIII convened a private council to give him its advice on the "question of Saint-Domingue." The council's unanimous recommendation was that

> It was time to reject all military expedition aiming to reconquer the old French colony because this would require the extermination of its entire population that was resolved to defend its liberty and its soil. . . . [Now] that the slave trade had been abolished, France would not be able to repopulate it, and it would be impossible to keep secret such an expedition that would require incalculable expenses and a prior consent from the parliamentary assemblies; that it would also be useless to think of a blockade of the ports because that would interfere with trade . . . and require the deployment of almost all of France's naval forces without any hope of success . . .; and finally that Boyer and his fellow citizens would throw themselves into the arms of the English if they felt threatened. (cited in Madiou 1988, 6: 193–194)

In a letter Thomas Clarkson also wrote to Boyer in May 1821, he told him that "[w]ith respect to France, it becomes you to be upon your guard. When I was at Paris last year, I understood that the French Government had given up all idea of trying to conquer Hayti by force of arms, but that they had not given up the idea of trying to obtain it by intrigue" (Clarkson 1952, 224–225).

Nothing had changed between 1821 and 1825 when Boyer accepted the ordinance. As for France's consideration of a massive military expedition like that of 1802, it had also become clear that given the balance of forces internationally at the time, it was no longer possible for France to reconquer its old colony militarily (Eugène 2003, 145–146). What changed, however, was that Boyer himself altered the terms of the negotiations with France. In April 1824 he sent two emissaries to France (Larose and Rouanez) with a letter to Esmangar that "left no doubt about the clauses of a treaty they were to conclude, and the indispensable formality of the recognition, by a royal ordinance, of our absolute independence from all foreign domination, of any sort of suzerainty, in a word, of the independence that we have enjoyed for the past twenty years" (*Pièces officielles* 1824, 7).

Boyer's "Instructions" stipulated the following acts to be included in the ordinance:

1) A royal ordinance that recognizes Haiti's independence from France; 2) Once the ordinance is obtained, Haiti will offer an indemnity to France to be paid in five installments, either in Haitian or foreign currency, or in equivalent Haitian goods; 3) French commercial ships will be admitted in all commercial ports of the Republic with the same privileges granted to other favored nations; 4) Crops produced in Haiti (sugar, coffee, cotton, indigo, cacao) and other commercial goods will not pay higher fees than those that French goods would pay in Haiti; 5) That Haiti will remain neutral in case of war between France and other powers; and 6) That Haiti would welcome a French chargé d'affaires or a general consul, and France will do the same for Haiti. (*Pièces officielles* 1824, 51–56; also cited in Coradin 1988, 164–165)

In 1825, France issued just such an ordinance, but with different stipulations concerning the amount of the indemnity (which Boyer's Instructions had not specified) and the tariff concessions Haiti would grant to France and those Haiti would pay to export goods to France. Given that to be the case, and that Mackau had signaled to Boyer that these terms could be renegotiated once the ordinance was accepted and ratified by Haiti, it would have been difficult if not impossible for Boyer to reject the ordinance he himself had requested. It is noteworthy that the baron de Las Casas, whom France sent to Haiti in 1837 along with Captain Charles Baudin and six naval war ships to threaten to blockade Haiti's ports if it did not honor its payments on the indemnity, admitted in his "Lettre tout à fait pour l'histoire" that Mackau's threat of a blockade in 1825 notwithstanding, Boyer accepted the ordinance only after he received the clarifications he had sought from the French emissary. Inginac also confirmed that this was the case. And Makau himself acknowledged in his report to the Minister of Marine and the Colonies that in his meeting with Boyer's emissaries (Inginac, Rouanez, and Frémont) the threat of a blockade did not have "any effect on them as did the assurance I gave them [about the ordinance] ... and this is so true that I could have succeeded better if I had never talked of the squadron" (of 14 war ships), but he did so because those were his orders (MAE/CP v. 7, 17 février 1838; Inginac 1843, 71; Mackau AP-156-1-20, 1825).

Boyer understood that the recognition of Haiti's independence stipulated in the third clause of the 1825 ordinance was conditional on Haiti paying off the indemnity in five years. He knew that this was impossible since he was compelled subsequently to borrow 30 million francs from a French bank at 80 percent to make the first payment in November 1825.[10] That transaction came to be known as the "double debt" Haiti incurred: the 150 million owed to France plus the 30 million from the French bank (Blancpain 2001, 66; Brière 2008, 162–163). Boyer set out immediately to renegotiate the amount of the indemnity and the other clauses of the 1825 ordinance dealing with trade, taxes, and duties to be paid to and received from France. Many attempts at such negotiations took place between 1825 and 1838.

But one set of events was significant and had to do with a renewed French threat of war if Haiti refused to honor its obligations under the 1825 ordinance. In 1830, the July Revolution (also known as the "Second French Revolution") forced King Charles X to abdicate power and was succeeded by his cousin Louis Philippe. In 1831 Boyer unilaterally eliminated the half duties exemption on French imports. France responded by threatening war. At the same time, Saint-Macary, the Haitian envoy Boyer had sent to France, signed two financial and trade treaties with France. The first treaty kept the original amount of the indemnity and required Haiti to pay 4 million francs per year until it was paid off, and it demanded that Haiti reimburse France for the duties it had collected in violation of the 1825 ordinance, namely, the half duties on Haitian exports since 1827, and the half duties on French imports since 1831. The second treaty eliminated the half duties but allowed French citizens to engage in wholesale and retail commerce in Haiti as well as own and/or inherit real estate properties, a clear violation of the 1805 Constitution. Boyer rejected both treaties and broke off diplomatic relations with France (Ardouin 1958, 10: 30–37; Madiou 1988, 7: 93–95; Brière 2008, 222–223).

Acting on instructions he received from France, Mollien, the French consul in Haiti, threatened military action against Haiti. Boyer responded by putting the army on alert. He also ordered the construction of a new city, Pétion-Ville, in the hills above Port-au-Prince and out of reach of French gunships, where government archives, military arsenals and supplies could be secured, and, if necessary, to relocate the seat of government (MAE 47CP, V, 19 juin 1831; Madiou 1988, 7: 97–104; Brière 2008, 219–225). The next major tension in Franco-Haitian relations came in November 1837 when France sent two commissioners, the baron de Las Casas and Captain Charles Baudin, and again threatened to blockade the ports of Haiti and Santo Domingo if Haiti did not pay the indemnity according to its means. Boyer again responded that Haiti was open to negotiating with France but would not do so under the threat of war and would defend its independence to the death (Madiou 1988, 7: 202–203; Brière 2008, 240–243).

As I mentioned earlier, by February 1838 Haiti and France signed two treaties. In the new treaties, France recognized Haiti as a free, sovereign, and independent state, and treated trade between the two countries on the same basis as those considered most favored nations. And the indemnity was reduced to 60 million francs to be paid in yearly installments over the next 30 years. But Haiti did not do so until 1883 (that is in 45 rather than 30 years) when President Lysius Salomon exclaimed that "I paid France the last term of the double debt of 1825" (cited in Turnier 1985, 27). The treaties also lowered the interest rate on the 30 million francs Haiti borrowed from a French bank to make the initial payment on the original 150 million francs indemnity from 6 to 3 percent. As such, the indemnity Haiti was now obligated to pay to France was reduced from 150 million to 90 million francs: the 30 million borrowed for the first installment in 1825 plus the 60 million agreed to in the 1838 treaties (MAE-CP v. 8, Ordonnance du Roi, 30 May 1838; Madiou 1988, 7: 214–215; Montague 1940, 85–87; Blancpain 2001, 63–74).

Boyer's gambit paid off, at least on the diplomatic front. By May 1826 Great Britain recognized Haiti's independence and sent a consul, Charles Mackenzie, to Haiti. Other European countries followed suit by sending their consuls to Haiti, including the free Hanseatic cities of Bremen and Hamburg, the Low Countries, Hanover, Prussia, Sweden, and Norway. In 1839, England invited Haiti to subscribe to the treaty it had concluded with France to suppress the slave trade, which Haiti did after France made the same request (Brière 2008,

154; Léger 1930, 201). Speaking about Haiti's international standing after 1825, A. N. Léger, who had been critical of Boyer's "capitulation" to France, admitted that "Europe was beginning to show particular interest to us. . . . The end of our quarrel with the old metropole was slowly making the horizon clearer. With international peace, we would be better able to mark our place in global activities" (1930, 201–202).

Based on the foregoing analysis, then, Boyer did not accept the 1825 ordinance because he feared war with France. This is so for two reasons. The first is that Boyer knew that France was not contemplating, preparing for, or capable of launching a massive military expedition to reconquer Haiti. The second is that although a blockade was an act of war and could have caused serious disruptions to international trade with Haiti, to be effective it would have needed to be expanded to all Haitian ports, and indeed throughout the entire island of Hispaniola (i.e., including the Spanish colony) that was under Boyer's control at the time. To do so, it would have been necessary for the French government to deploy a much larger French fleet "without any guarantee of success," as the independent council appointed by Louis XVIII had concluded in 1821. There was no evidence that France was preparing for or capable of doing so, and that is probably why Mackau remarked in his report (cited above) that Boyer's emissaries did not seem concerned about his mention of a blockade.

If the fear of war was not the principal reason Boyer agreed to pay the indemnity, two others were. The first, as I have argued, was the desperate need for Boyer to gain official recognition of Haiti's independence by other powers and become accepted as a legitimate nation. But those powers, especially the major Western powers and the United States, maintained their solidarity with France and refused to do so first. The second reason also had to do with legitimacy, namely, that of private property ownership. Beaubrun Ardouin was one of the historians of the times who understood the reasons Pétion and Boyer made their offers of a quid pro quo to France to recognize Haiti's independence in return for an indemnity for the former colonial property owners.

Many have argued, Ardouin pointed out, that the colonial property owners, or their heirs, had no right to receive an indemnity for the loss of their properties, and neither should France in return for its recognition of Haiti's independence because the horrible and criminal colonial regime forced

Haitians to take up arms to win their freedom and their independence, and therefore had the right to exclude the colonialists and their ilk among them. All that is true, he maintained, because the right to independence is indisputable, as is that of excluding the former colonists to preserve Haiti's liberties (1958, 8: 23–24). But, he countered, enlightened "men" must preserve what is sacred.

> And **property** is one such case because it is really the basis of all social order, old or new. A colony founded by a nation can resist oppression by its metropolitan power, take up arms against it, conquer its country to become a free, distinct, and independent and sovereign people, and exercise all rights over all goods in that country; but on the condition that it respects all that concerns the private rights of individuals.
>
> However, if, motivated by political considerations this new people deem it necessary to exclude certain private individuals from its midst, it has the right to do so; but it is obligated to indemnify them for the properties they owned legally, and which had been taken from them by necessity. Because all rights demand a corrective duty; otherwise, it is not a right, but violence, which can only be fought against and annihilated by a superior force. (Ibid., emphasis in the original)

It would have been useful to enunciate these principles, Ardouin went on to say to "prove the injustice of the critiques of Pétion for having proposed the indemnity: those who advanced these criticisms failed to think through that question." But what gave a country the right to possess colonies in the first place? Ardouin did not consider that question, but it lies at the heart of the matter here. Had he done so, he would perhaps have realized that the colonists whose properties he believed should be indemnified because they were taken from them by force had themselves not only expropriated the lands of the indigenous Taino population of Ayiti but exterminated them. That genocide was first carried out by the Spanish who were subsequently displaced by the French when they took possession of the western third of Hispaniola and renamed it Saint-Domingue. They then brought slaves from Africa to labor on their plantations, and whose revolution in 1791 ended that criminal and brutal system.

What "sacred" principle of property applied then other than that of "might makes right"? B. Vendryes, a former colonist, expressed that point succinctly:

Saint-Domingue, this island of Haiti, had its part in the cruelty and injustice of which America was the theater and the victim.

From the first days of its discovery, Christopher Columbus had been held accountable and sent to Spain.

It was for this that a venerable bishop, Barthelemy de Las Cazas (sic), in his ill-considered pity, thought to buy African slaves. A vain and fatal measure! These poor, harmless, even hospitable inhabitants of Haiti disappeared no less to the last man, and 30 million (sic) of Africa's children perished in the fields of America.

The buccaneers, these bandits that we could not hate, committed atrocious crimes against the Spaniards in Saint-Domingue, these victims we could not feel sorry for.

If Saint-Domingue achieved a high degree of prosperity, it is due in part to the slave trade, until recently an object of the ambition of France and England, encouraged by the laws of the time, justly done away with, and considered criminal by current laws.

Their fortunes only lasted so long: the Constituent Assembly started it, the Convention hastened it,[11] and the empire completed the ruin of the old colonists of Saint-Domingue. (Vendryes 1839, 1–2; also cited in Joachim 1971, 360–361; addition mine)

It is clear, then, that the "sacred principle" of private property that Ardouin was referring to is neither inviolable by those who believe in it when it serves their purpose, nor is it the foundation of all social order (in place and time). It is, however, the fundamental principle of bourgeois society. As Marx has shown in Volume One of *Capital* (1976), without private property in land, labor could not be expropriated and prevented from having access to the means of production and self-reproduction; there could be no production of surplus value (profit) by the laborer and no accumulation of capital (wealth) by and for the capitalist. In short, there would be no capitalism.

Returning to Ardouin and his attempt to justify Pétion's (and subsequently Boyer's) offer of the indemnity for the former colonial owners, he takes the latter's right to private property as a given and not as an expression in law of a set of relations of power and of production in time and place for the benefit of those who own or appropriate such properties to use them to extract wealth or resources from those excluded from access to those properties. That is why he concluded his remarks on the indemnity by saying that by offering it, Pétion (and hence Boyer) "acted in the real interest of the people" (1958, 8: 23–24). Yet, he himself documented the opposite, namely, that the policies of all the rulers from Toussaint Louverture to Jean-Pierre Boyer (and since) prioritized their own interests and those of the dominant classes who benefited the most from the confiscation and redistribution of the colonial properties, albeit to a less extreme extent under Pétion, and who used the power of the state to compel the laborers to work on them.

Be that as it may, the key issue here is that Pétion and Boyer, both of whom (and their predecessors) believed in the bourgeois right to private property ownership, sought to legitimize the redistribution of the properties expropriated from the old colonial property owners to create a new landed class in Haiti. And they saw no other way to do that than by offering to pay an indemnity to the former colonial owners. I agree with Jean-François Brière that accepting to pay the indemnity was not the price paid for the recognition of Haiti only, but "was in reality a massive transfer of property to the mulatto and black elite" (2008, 156; AE-B-III-380, 25 Février 1826). Jean Coradin came to a similar conclusion: "The Ordonnance of 17 April, by abdicating French sovereignty over its old colony, virtually ratified the ownership by Haitians of the properties of the former colonials" (1988, 202). Paul Cheney made the same point when he wrote that the "indemnity paid to the former plantations owners of Saint-Domingue can be seen, from a certain perspective, as a gentlemen's agreement between successive landholding elites" (2017, 211). Similarly, Jean Casimir noted that "the transfer of ownership over the territory from the mother country was so important that, despite the consciousness of their victory over the French expeditionary army, these former guarantors of the colonial order took the initiative to offer the imperial power a fabulous sum of money to compensate it for the loss of this property" (2020, 94). In a disingenuous, yet partly true, diplomatic note he sent to Boyer, King Louis Philippe, who himself had threatened military action against Haiti for not honoring its debt obligations, remarked that "If the indemnity was the price for the recognition of Haiti, the King's government, as much in consideration of the Haitian nation as for the respect for the rights of peoples, could have relinquished it; but it was accepted for the respect of private property" (cited in Ardouin 1958: 8, 24, n.1).[12]

The expropriated colonial property owners, however, saw this agreement differently, namely, that by accepting the indemnity and refusing to reconquer Haiti so they could regain their properties, their own government had betrayed them, and they were the major losers in this deal. This was because the real value of their properties in 1791 had been estimated at 350 million francs, that is, two and one third times more than the 150 million indemnity that was based on the value of the revenues of their properties in 1789 (Eugène 2003, 143). Désiré Dalloz and associates, consultants, and advocates for the dispossessed colonial property owners, offered one of the clearest explanations of the meaning and implications of the indemnity. First, in recognizing Haiti's independence, it made it possible for it to henceforth gain the recognition of the other imperial powers, which had hitherto refused to do so before France, and to establish normal diplomatic and commercial relations with them (and other nations). Haiti's status therefore changed from a de facto to a legitimate and rightfully independent nation (Dalloz et al. 1829, 20). This was a primary objective of all Haiti's rulers since independence, from Dessalines to Boyer, all of whom categorically rejected any form of French suzerainty as nonnegotiable.

Second, the indemnity settled the question of property once and for all in favor of the Haitian ruling class. It is true, Dalloz et al. argued, that the 1825 Ordinance does not mention the transfer of the private properties of the former colonial owners. Nonetheless, this is what the ordinance did, both in terms of the properties that were sold or given to private individuals by the Haitian state, and those that became part of the national domain, that is, public property. The indemnity that the Haitian government agreed to pay, then, was to ensure that the ordinance that also recognized its independence was simultaneously a "transfer of the property titles henceforth nontransferable and free from all French inheritance in Saint-Domingue." In other words, with the ordinance, the French government legalized "the dispossession of the former colonists which implied the voluntary renunciation of their properties" (Dalloz et al. 1829, 19–30; also cited in Coradin 1988, 202).

DEBT, POLITICS, AND DEVELOPMENT
The 90 million francs indemnity (60 million plus the 30 million borrowed in 1825 for the first payment on the original 150 million francs) that was finally paid off in 1883 represented about 10 years of fiscal receipts for the Haitian government, heavily dependent as it was on customs duties for its revenue. Some, like Jacques Barros (1984), Leslie Péan (2000), Itazienne Eugène

(2003), Paul Farmer (2003), Frédérique Beauvois (2009), Anthony Phillips (2009), Eddy Toussaint (Tontongi 2010), and Porter et al. (2022) have argued that the indemnity and the burdens it inflicted on Haiti were a root cause of its inability to develop its economy since 1825.

Barros believed that the indemnity had serious consequences for all sectors of the Haitian economy (203). Farmer thought that its "impact on nineteenth century Haiti was devastating" (7), whereas Péan said that it was the principal cause of Haiti's inability to develop its economy in the nineteenth century or since because it prevented the government from being able to lay the "foundation for an accumulation that could have led to some type of development" (245). For Phillips, the "independence debt drained the Haitian treasury of its capital. The Haitian economy—ravaged by war and long cut off from export markets—could not generate enough revenue to support the Debt" (7-8). For Beauvois, the indemnity "devastated the economy of the young republic.... [It] became hostage to the debt ... and [it] was a clear strategy by the old metropolitan power to maintain its unofficial hegemony on the rebellious colony [and] place [Haiti] under France's economic grasp" (119). For Eddy Toussaint (alias Tontongi), "the indemnity irreversibly affected Haiti's development by putting the country in a vicious circle of indebtedness, impoverishment, authoritarianism, and dependence on the imperialist powers, notably France and the United States." (2). And as Porter et al.'s "The Ransom" report put it, "The double debt helped push Haiti into a cycle of debts that hobbled the country for more than 100 years, draining away much of its revenue and chopping away its ability to build the essential institutions and infrastructure of an independent nation."

It is undeniable that the indemnity was harmful, insofar as it saddled a country with limited resources to paying a debt that was agreed to by its rulers (Pétion and Boyer) for their benefit and those of the ruling class to which they belonged because this was a decision in which the people had no say, and whose exploitation they believed would generate income not only for the property owners, but for the government as well in the form of taxes. The indemnity debt was unpopular among many sectors of the population and sparked protests in Port-au-Prince and an uprising in Cap Haïtien that were quickly suppressed. That was also the case in Santo Domingo where the Boyer regime met with widespread opposition from farmers and merchants who were compelled to pay taxes on crops for domestic consumption and for export. There is no doubt, as A. N. Léger mentioned earlier, that those policies played a role in the uprising against Boyer in 1843.

It is worth noting, however, that in the Acte de Déchéance (Bill of Impeachment) issued by the leaders who led the uprising against Boyer in March 1843, no mention was made of the indemnity among the charges brought against him. Rather, the Acte accused him of cronyism and abuse of power and that he removed senators from office illegally, selected candidates for the Senate who would do his bidding, usurped his authority to pardon and issue paper money, compelled the Senate to grant him powers he did not have under the constitution to form an army or to change the monetary system and suspend civil laws, unilaterally changed the tax laws, changed laws and refused to observe those enacted by the Senate, denied citizens access to due process and judges and subjected them to arbitrary judgments by civil or military commissions he controlled, removed judges arbitrarily and replaced them with those loyal to him, and arbitrarily fired civil employees and public functionaries (cited in Madiou 1988, 7: 474).

Contrary to the authors mentioned above, then, I agree with Alain Turnier (1985, 27–42) that the "double" indemnity debt was not the primary cause of Haiti's inability to develop its economy in the nineteenth century. Instead, I contend that two other factors played a more significant role. The first had to do with the inability of the Haitian ruling class to expropriate and proletarianize the former slaves and their descendants since the time of Louverture. And the second resulted from the internecine conflicts between different factions of the postindependence ruling class to control the state since the assassination of Dessalines in 1806 and their dealings with foreign capital and governments, including incurring even more egregious debts than the indemnity that they could not repay.[13]

As mentioned previously, the respective governments of Dessalines, Pétion, Christophe, and Boyer tried to revitalize the plantation system that had made Saint-Domingue the most productive sugar-producing colony in the eighteenth century and to transform the former slave masses and their descendants into wage laborers to work on them, whether they were paid wages or in kind, or a combination of both. But they all failed to do so on a scale large enough to restore the plantations and reach their previous levels of productivity. The former slaves and their descendants fought against the consolidation of landed property by the dominant classes and succeeded in gaining access to land and their own means of production and reproduction by producing food crops for their own consumption as well as for the local, national, and world markets. Consequently, as Jean Casimir put it,

> the plantation disappeared as the foundational institution in the economic landscape. The basis of structural dependence was swept away. The prior invisibility of the workers reduced to slavery, and of their conditions of existence, produced a blindness among those who took over the positions of the oligarchy. Work itself, and its autonomous potential, became invisible. The oligarchy perceived the forms of existence that flourished outside the capitalism of the commodity-producing plantations as simply the expression of varieties of laziness, idleness, and vagabondage. They repeated the unrealizable dream of large-scale agriculture, which governed the political discourse of the nineteenth-century, with exhaustive monotony. (2020, 97–98)

Three categories of landed peasant farmers emerged: those who owned land (i.e., had legal titles), those who possessed but did not own land (i.e., had de facto but not de jure ownership), and those who leased land through the métayage or sharecropping system from large landowners. Those peasant farmers who owned/possessed land were also those who had larger, though still relatively small farms of approximately four to seven hectares (1 ha = 2.5 acres). Though there are no precise data on their percentage of the farming population, the "middle class" landowners/possessors were a minority among the peasantry as a whole and were generally more secure financially and more independent because they also owned their tools, equipment, and draft animals. The second category of peasant farmers, who comprised the majority, were those who could be considered the "small" peasants. They did not have land titles but possessed them and enjoyed full rights to their lands. They could not sell those lands but could bequeath or sell the "right of possession" to others. The lands these farmers possessed were not always contiguous and were also parceled out to several inheritors, thereby fragmenting them into even smaller plots.

The third category of peasants were either tenant farmers or sharecroppers (métayers) who leased land from the landed bourgeoisie (i.e., properties larger than 25 ha or 63 acres) who subdivided their estates into smaller units, or even from the "middle class" landowners. The distinction between tenant farmer and sharecropper is important because whereas the former tended to pay a fix rent to the landowner in advance for a year or more, sharecroppers paid their rent in money or in kind at the time of the harvest, and their rents tended to be higher than those of the tenant farmers. It could be said, then, that sharecroppers were more exploited by the landowners than were the tenant farmers, though either of them could be evicted for nonpayment of the rents (Moral 1961, 179–181; Bellande et al. 1980, 33–42; Girault 1981, 95–97; Barros 1984, 1: 385–388; Luc 1976, 36; Lundahl 1979, 264; Joachim 1979, 126; Millet 1978, 18–21; Léopold-Hector 1977, 6–7; Dartigue 1938, 37; Dupuy 1989, 99–103).

It is worth noting here that the system of tenant farming or sharecropping could have been the basis for the emergence of capitalist farmers sensu stricto and the creation of a domestic market to produce food crops as well as agricultural equipment, machinery, and consumer goods. Both the tenant farmer and the landowner would have an interest in increasing production for the domestic and export markets to make more profits and accumulate more capital. For the tenant farmer, higher crop yields and revenues would have required the introduction of better tools and equipment in the production process, in other words, labor-saving technologies, and for the landowner it would have meant raising the rents to the tenant farmers. That alternative never materialized. One reason was that the sharecroppers and those small peasants with access to land would have needed to be expropriated to create a larger farming population without access to land alongside those who were already landless and hired themselves out as day laborers. Another factor against the introduction of more advanced labor-saving technology was the relatively small size and noncontiguous or fragmented configuration of the farms. Farmland, in other words, would have needed to be consolidated to make the cost of producing and buying labor-saving technologies worthwhile, all of which would also have necessitated the expropriation of the small landowners/possessors especially. As Marx pointed out,

> Where capital has not yet taken over agriculture, a large proportion of agricultural produce is still used directly as means of subsistence and not as commodities. In that event a large proportion of the working population will not have been transformed into wage-labourers and a large proportion of the conditions of labour will not yet have become capital. (1976 1: 950–951)

Achieving these transformations in turn would have necessitated a relatively stable government capable of planning, legislating, and investing public resources and revenues to achieve these desired ends. As Robert Fatton explained it, Haiti needed what he called an "integral state" that could

> organize both the political unity of the different factions of the ruling class and the "organic relations between political society and civil society." It contains social conflicts within constitutional limits and manages processes of class formation, struggles, and compromises. Ultimately, it expresses the hegemonic governance of the ruling class—the capacity to command effectively without permanent resort to brute force. (2007, 82)

Without such an "integral state," Fatton goes on to say, "politics tends to become predatory and chaotic" as well as despotic (Ibid., 83). That is exactly what came to be in Haiti: a ruling class at war with itself with different factions vying for access to control the state and the prebends or fiscal benefits it yielded. Given that most of the rural population were farmers with access to land, they controlled the means and processes of production, and hence the rate of their exploitation. This was the case even where the landed bourgeoisie tried to extract more surplus from the sharecroppers.[14] Second, unable to defeat the majority of the peasantry, expropriate, and proletarianize them, the bourgeoisie was stymied in its efforts in the mid-nineteenth century to develop a national infrastructure in both the rural and urban areas; expand public, technical, and professional education; diversify agriculture; promote the growth of small and medium-size industries; establish a textile industry; and create a coastal maritime service, among other ventures (Bellegarde 1938, 121–124; Moore 1972, 31; Turnier 1985, 211–218; Dupuy 1989, 96–113).

Consequently, the dominant classes were limited to accumulating wealth primarily from the circulation rather than the production process. They became a commercial and a rentier bourgeoisie that engaged in financial, commercial, and trade relations with other countries to which they could export Haitian agricultural products (principally coffee, lumber), and from which they could import durable and consumer goods they resold on the domestic market.

In addition to commercial enterprises and/or land as the basis of wealth accumulation, the state, and the prebends it yielded to those in power, became a source of enrichment for those who controlled it but lacked the assets and means of production (land, businesses) of those in the private sector.[15] Its bureaucratic, police, and military apparatuses also created their own system of clientelism and mechanism of wealth appropriation. Moreover, since the presidency also controlled the other branches of the state such as the legislature, the judicial, and civil service bureaucracies in addition to the military and police, the tendency of those in power was to prolong their hold on that office as much as possible. Dictatorship and rule by force, then, became the only form of government possible under such circumstances, and "revolutions" or coups d'état became the principal means of making and unmaking governments. That explains why between 1804 and 1915, out of the 24 heads of state in 111 years, 13 were overthrown by force, three were killed while in office, six died in office, and two completed their terms (Dupuy 1989, 115–123).

The weakness, divisions, and endless conflicts among factions of the ruling class to control the state made them also vulnerable to manipulation and exploitation by foreign capital and their governments and facilitated their dominance over the Haitian economy. Successive governments or would-be heads of state sought the support of foreign governments by making concessions to them and/or borrowing large sums of money from foreign banks. For example, President Fabre-Nicolas Geffrard (1859–1867) turned to England for its support against Sylvain Salnave who was seeking to overthrow him. When Salnave became president from 1867–1869, he offered to let the United States establish a naval station at the Môle Saint-Nicolas (on the northwest coast) in return for its support against Nissage Saget who succeeded in overthrowing him. When Michel Domingue took power in 1874, he offered to let England establish a protectorate at the Môle in exchange for its support. When Lysius Salomon succeeded him in 1879 he promised the Môle along with the Île de la Tortue (off the north central coast) to the United States in return for its military support while he called on France to establish a protectorate over Haiti. President François Légitime, who lasted one year in office (1788–1789), was said to have offered the Môle to the French while Florvil Hyppolite, who overthrew Légitime and ruled for eight years (1888–1896), sought the support of the United States. No actual land concessions were ever made but heads or would-be heads of state used them as bargaining chips with foreign powers, all of which weakened them (Dupuy 1989, 126).

More serious and consequential than the never-materialized offers of territorial concessions, however, were the borrowings of large sums of money from foreign banks that opened the way for foreign capital to reassert its dominance over Haiti's economy. The most notorious of those financial transactions occurred with the so-called Domingue loan contracted with a French bank in 1874 for 15 million francs at 33 percent (meaning that Haiti received only 10 million). Unable to meet the two-year repayment terms, the Domingue government took out another loan for 50 million francs allegedly to consolidate the first loan with that of the "double" indemnity debt (the balance on which, in 1876, was 7.76 million francs with interest according to Turnier (1985, 27). In 1896, the government of T. Antoine Sam borrowed another 50 million francs, and again, with those loans not repaid, the government of Antoine Simon borrowed another 65 million francs at an annual rate of 5 percent to be paid in five years.

As Pierre-Charles summed it, between 1875 and 1910 Haiti borrowed a total of 166 million francs, "half of which were kept by the lenders under various pretexts.... In all in 1914 Haiti's total foreign debt amounted to 113,156,500 francs.... [And] it was not only foreign bankers who enriched themselves, but also many functionaries who confused the interests of the state with their own." These debts were not fully repaid until 1961 (1967, 136–137). Moreover, it is worth noting the evolution of the ratio of these debts to Haiti's treasury, whose principal source of foreign currency came from its exports. According to Turnier, for every three dollars Haiti earned on its coffee exports in 1875, $0.33 went to service the foreign debt. That increased to $1.20 in 1896, and $1.00 in 1910 (1985, 35). Looked at differently, the burden of repaying Haiti's foreign debts was not caused primarily by the indemnity but by subsequent debts accrued after 1875 for reasons other than repaying the indemnity when the ratio of the debt repayment rose from 11 percent of revenue before 1875 to 40 percent in 1875, and to 30 percent in 1910.

I agree with Péan who observed that because of these practices, the Haitian state became "a vulgar agent for the condottieri of international trade and finance" (2000, 266). As Benoit Joachim noted, these onerous practices explain why none of the governments that succeeded Boyer sought to renegotiate or invalidate the indemnity, despite their criticisms of him for having agreed to this "shameful tribute." Instead, they all agreed to repay the indemnity, even at the cost of great difficulties ... not because they believed it was fair to indemnify the former colonialists, [but] to curry the favors of the French governments, and to live in peace with the France they all venerated. Because the interests [of the rulers of Haiti] did not coincide with those of most of the nation, the ruling classes often gave in to the pressures exercised by the metropolitan rulers, even without any significant strengthening of relations between the two countries. (1971, 364)

By the beginning of the twentieth century, and because of these self-serving political transactions, foreign banking capital had reestablished its control over the national economy, which in turn facilitated the return of foreign commercial and industrial capital. Laws that before 1843 protected the interests of Haitian merchants by limiting the rights and activities of foreigners (such as the prohibition against buying and owning real estate, limiting foreign trade to designated port cities, buying coffee and other crops only from Haitian merchants, buying and selling wholesale only, and paying high fees to trade) had since been gradually relaxed or changed or not enforced. Once that happened, it was no longer foreigners residing in Haiti and married to Haitians who could evade those restrictions. Foreign merchants now began to establish their businesses directly in Haiti and displace Haitians, even though that process was uneven and localized in certain port cities. These changes soon opened the way for direct foreign capital investment in production resulting from land concessions to European firms who began to produce and process coffee, cacao, vanilla, pineapples, rubber, and lumber. As I will show in the next chapter, the United States invasion and occupation of Haiti from 1915 to 1934 would complete that process. During and after the Occupation, the Haitian currency, the gourde, would henceforth be pegged to the US dollar rather than the French franc, and the United States became the single most important market for Haitian exports and imports, and the unquestionably dominant power broker in Haiti.

CONCLUSION
From the foregoing analysis, then, the following conclusion can be drawn. First, President Boyer, as had his predecessor Alexandre Pétion, did not offer to pay an indemnity to France because he/they feared French military aggression. They both knew that France was not preparing to send or capable of

sending a massive, Napoleonesque military expedition to reconquer its former colony at the time (1814–1838). Pétion and Boyer did so instead to solve two problems simultaneously: the recognition of Haiti's independence and to settle once and for all the property question in the interest of the Haitian ruling class, even if some may not have understood it as such. That is why no government since Boyer contested the legitimacy of the 1825 Ordinance or the debts Haiti incurred to pay the indemnity. Former president Aristide was the only head of state to demand restitution from France for the indemnity on the ground that France imposed the indemnity on his nineteenth-century predecessors and compelled Boyer to accept the ordinance or face military reprisals if he refused. As I have shown, however, that argument does not stand up to scrutiny. Pétion put that offer on the table first, and Boyer brought it to a conclusion. They both acted on their own agency, in the respective domestic and international contexts and constraints they confronted, to advance what they believed to be in the interest of the nation they governed, but which also coincided first and foremost with the interests of their class: the question of property.

Second, as onerous as it was for the treasury, the indemnity was not the principal cause of Haiti's inability to develop its economy in the nineteenth century. The key determining factors were, on the one hand, the inability of the Haitian ruling class to expropriate and proletarianize the former slaves and their descendants who had gained access to land of their own, revitalize the plantation system and lay the ground for a more widespread infrastructural and capitalist development and, on the other hand, the internecine conflicts among different factions of the ruling class to control the apparatuses of the state as a means of enrichment through corruption and cronyism.[16]

Third, the indemnity, and the moneys borrowed to repay it along with other loans incurred for different reasons, gave rise to nefarious practices among post-Boyer heads of state of borrowing more and larger sums of money from foreign bankers that increasingly taxed their ability to repay those debts. In addition to embezzling parts of those moneys for self-enrichment, these obligations weakened the governing classes and facilitated the return and dominance of foreign financial, commercial, and industrial capital, which in turn solidified Haiti's uneven development as a supplier of cheap labor and an exporter of agricultural crops, raw materials, manufactured goods, and labor. As Turnier summed it up succinctly: "to stop the descent into hell, good will, competence, and patriotism were not enough, and foreign aid was essential, whereas imperialism aimed to carve-up its prey. External finance succeeded in transferring to the economy the colonialism that was politically defeated on the battlefields of Saint-Domingue, and thus perpetuate the past" (1985, 40).

NOTES

1. This chapter is a revised version of Chapter Four, "Property, Debt, and Development: Rethinking the Indemnity Question," in Alex Dupuy, *Rethinking the Haitian Revolution: Slavery, Independence, and the Struggle for Recognition* (Lanham, MD: Rowman & Littlefield, 2019), 91–133.

2. Boyer was referring to unresolved negotiations that had been ongoing since 1814 when Pétion first raised the issue of paying an indemnity to compensate the former colonial property owners, which I will discuss below.

3. These instructions were contained in a letter the Comte de Chabrol, the Minister of Marine, and the Colonies gave to Mackau before he left France (AP/15/1/20, 17 Avril 1825).

4. The "Praslin" uprising is so called because it was planned on the Praslin plantation in Les Cayes.

5. Much of the following section is derived from Dupuy 1989, 55–91.

6. Many functionaries and military officers took advantage of their positions to plunder the public treasury, steal the pay of soldiers, and dispossess citizens of their properties among other forms of embezzlement. So widespread were these practices that Dessalines was said to have told his officials that they "could pluck the chicken but don't make it crow" (cited in Bellegarde 1938, 92).

7. In 1810, General André Rigaud returned to Haiti from France and was named General of Division by Pétion. He subsequently tried to wrest control of the South from Pétion. Rigaud died in 1812, and General Borgella took control temporarily but submitted to Pétion's forces in 1812 (Ardouin 1958, 7: 71–113).

8. There is some confusion on Medina's death. Wallez claimed he died in jail from his illness (Wallez 1826, 16). Ardouin and Madiou said he was killed (Madiou 1988, V: 268; Ardouin 1958, 8: 15).

9. By which Pétion meant the dispossessed colonial property owners.

10. Borrowing the money at 80 percent meant that Haiti received only 24 million francs, with the balance due in 25 years at 6 percent interest per year.

11. Vendryes was obviously referring to the National Assembly that formed the first government of the French Revolution in 1789, and the National Convention that abolished slavery in 1794.

12. It is worth noting here that in 1838 the French king acknowledged and contradicted what the Debray *Rapport* hid behind cowardly to dismiss Aristide's demand for *restitution*, namely, the claim that the "rights of peoples to self-determination" was not recognized at the time. From my standpoint, however, Aristide's demand is unfounded not because it does not have legal standing but because it was offered as a *quid pro quo* by Pétion and seen through its conclusion by Boyer in the interest of the Haitian bourgeoisie.

13. The following segments are derived from Dupuy 1989, 99–129 and Dupuy 2014, 54–62.

14. Sharecroppers didn't own the land they worked and live on, but they owned the tools and animals, and hence controlled when and how they worked.

15. The term "prebend" is adapted from Max Weber, who used it to refer to those who hold public office "as a source of the official's private income." As he also put it, "prebends" or a "prebendal organization" refers to "the official rent payment for life, payments which are somehow fixed to the objects or which are essentially *economic* usufruct from land or other sources. They must be compensated for the fulfillment of actual or fictitious office duties; they are goods permanently set aside for the economic assurance of the office" (Weber 1946, 206–207). Weber formulated this concept of prebendal appropriation to analyze practices that originated in feudal societies, and especially in those societies like France and England where the purchase of office became institutionalized and continued into the early nineteenth century. I am using it here to describe how the holders of public office in Haiti, especially, but not limited to the executive branch of government, transformed those offices into sources of personal income and enrichment, thereby institutionalizing corruption as a form of prebendal income.

16. For the most comprehensive analysis of the "political economy of corruption" in Haiti, see Leslie Péan (2000, 2005, 2006, 2007).

2

The US Occupation, Foreign Capital, and Transformation of the Haitian Economy[1]

INTRODUCTION

In a bold Op-Ed he wrote on April 18, 1998 titled "Foreign Affairs; Techno Nothings," *The New York Times* columnist Thomas Friedman criticized the executives at Silicon Valley for failing to understand and appreciate the global geopolitical context in which they are operating, and the role the U.S. government plays in making it possible for their firms to "carry digital voices, videos and data farther and faster around the world, all the trade and financial integration [they are] promoting through innovation, and all the wealth [they] are generating." All this is happening, Friedman argued, "in a world stabilized by a benign superpower called the United States of America. The hidden hand of the global market would never work without the hidden fist. And the hidden fist that keeps the world safe for Silicon Valley's technologies to flourish is called the United States Army, Air Force, Navy, and Marine Corps (with the help, incidentally, of global institutions like the UN and the International Monetary Fund)" (Friedman 1998, 13).

There are two points I thought were remarkable about this Op-Ed. The first was how rare it is to see a columnist for a major newspaper like *The New York Times* make such a clear connection between the use of military power and the global expansion and profitability of capitalist firms. The second is the conundrum critics like Friedman face when they try to justify the use of such power to advance U.S. business interests. On the one hand, because he believes in the virtues of the market, globalization, and free trade, but realizes that this requires a stable world order made possible and kept open using force, he characterizes that force as benign. On the other hand, he understands that those who don't believe in the imperatives of the capitalist market system or the hegemony of the United States in enforcing its rules may have to be compelled to do so by force, which, in such a case, would not be hidden or benign but openly violent and repressive. Friedman illustrated this dilemma in an exchange he reported having with an IBM executive who said that they were not loyal to the United States only because they see themselves as "IBM U.S., IBM Canada, IBM Australia, IBM China." And to which Friedman responded, "Well, the next time Congress closes another military base in Asia, call Microsoft's navy to secure the sea lanes of Asia" (Ibid.).

Contrary to Friedman, however, force is needed not only to maintain the world safe for capitalism but was in fact the sine qua non to its emergence as a world system in the late fifteenth century. The capitalist world market and economy did not emerge historically from what Adam Smith called the natural propensity of human beings to truck, barter, and trade, but was created through the barrel of a gun. It was the military superiority of Western Europe that made possible the conquest and colonization of peoples around the world, and the genocides they engendered from the Americas to the Indian subcontinent, Asia, and Africa from the fifteenth to the early twentieth centuries. Smith himself understood this contradiction in 1776 when he published *The Wealth of Nations* in a way that Friedman, writing in 1998, had not. After discussing the historical significance of the discovery of America and that of the passage to the East Indies by way of the Cape of Good Hope, Smith offered this conclusion: "By uniting, in some measure, the most distant parts of the world, by enabling them to relieve one another's wants, to increase one another's enjoyments, and to encourage one another's industry, their general tendency would seem to be beneficial. To the natives, however, both of the East and West Indies, all the commercial benefits which can have resulted from those events have been sunk and lost in the dreadful misfortune which they have occasioned" (Smith 1998, 363–364).

Smith's point may be expressed another way: the freedom of capital to move around the world required then and requires now the subjection of others and the bloody suppression of those who stand in its way. It is in this context that I would like to look at the role that military power played in the rise of the United States as an industrial power in the late nineteenth century and where the occupation of Haiti from 1915 to 1934 fits into that process. This will also allow me to analyze how that occupation contributed to and exacerbated the underdevelopment of the Haitian economy since 1915.

This essay has three sections. The first will focus on the principal objectives of the occupation: to substitute the political and economic dominance of the United States for that of its European rivals (France in particular) during the nineteenth century; to create the conditions for the investment of U.S. capital by expropriating peasants and farmers from their land and proletarianizing them; and to install compliant heads of state to run the country, and create a new Haitian army and police to maintain order after the U.S. forces withdrew from Haiti in 1934.

The second section covers the period from 1934 to 1986 and centers on two principal developments. The first deals with the continuing processes of proletarianization of Haitian workers and the investment of U.S. and Canadian capital in agricultural and industrial, primarily extractive, production. And the second analyzes the struggles between mulatto and black factions of the Haitian bourgeoisie and middle class to control the state and its apparatuses. The Occupation authorities had favored the former, who became heads of state and high-ranking officers in the new Haitian army. These trends challenged the traditional means of social promotion for sectors of the black bourgeoisie and middle class who tended to occupy these key positions during the nineteenth and early twentieth centuries, thereby reigniting the "color question" as the central ideological rallying cry of those factions. That struggle culminated in the rise of François Duvalier to the presidency in 1957, the brutal 29-year dictatorship he installed that ended in 1986 when his son, Jean-Claude, who succeeded him in 1971, was overthrown.

The third section, from 1986 to the present, deals with the popular movement for a democratic alternative after Jean-Claude Duvalier's ouster and exile to France, and led to the election of the then Liberation Theology priest Jean-Bertrand Aristide to the presidency in 1990. Promising to challenge the rule of the bourgeoisie, disband the Haitian army, and reject the neo-liberal economic policies the United States and the international financial institutions (IFIs)—the World Bank, the International Monetary Fund, and the Inter-American Bank for Development Bank—devised for Haiti in favor of more progressive and redistributive domestic policies, Aristide was overthrown by the military seven months after taking office in February 1991.

Though he showed signs of reneging on his populist agenda before his overthrow, Aristide abandoned them when U.S. president Bill Clinton returned him to Haiti in October 1994 accompanied by 20,000 U.S. Marines. As a quid pro quo for his return, Aristide faithfully implemented the neoliberal economic policies devised by the IFIs, including lowering the tariffs on rice imports to 3 percent, thereby ending Haiti's self-sufficiency in rice production in favor of cheaper imports from the United States.

Aristide and his successors to the presidency, including his short-lived second term (2001–2004), and those who came to power before and after the devastating earthquake that struck Haiti in 2010, pursued the same policies to preserve Haiti's "comparative advantage" as the lowest-paid labor force for the textile assembly industries in the Caribbean and Central America.

I: THE OCCUPATION AND THE FIRST PHASE OF TRANSFORMATION: 1915–1934

The U.S. invasion and occupation of Haiti must be understood in the context of the projection of its power in Central America and the Caribbean to displace its European rivals, establish its hegemony, and facilitate the penetration of U.S. capital throughout the region and beyond since the mid-nineteenth century. Far from being peaceful or benign, as Friedman argued, this process was imperial and violent, characterized by military interventions in and occupations of many countries in the region. They included Nicaragua in 1853, 1854, 1857, 1894, 1898, 1899, 1910, 1912–1925, and 1926–1933; Honduras in 1903, 1907, 1911, 1912, 1919, 1924, and 1925; Guatemala in 1920; Mexico in 1859, 1866, 1870, 1873, 1876, 1913, 1914–1917, and 1918–1919; Cuba in 1906–1909, 1912, 1917–1922, and 1933; the Dominican Republic in 1903, 1904, 1914, and 1916–1924; and Haiti in 1888, 1891, 1914, and 1915–1934. The United States acquired the Virgin Islands from Denmark in 1916 after threatening to seize them if the Danish government refused to sell them (Dupuy 1989, 130).

Walter LaFeber summed up the process of the imperial ascendancy of the United States in the region since the mid-nineteenth century succinctly:

> Monroe and Adams had originally intended [the Monroe Doctrine] to protect Latin American revolutions from outside (that is, European)

interference. Eighty years later the power balance had shifted to the United States, and the Doctrine itself shifted to mean that Latin America should now be controlled by outside (that is, North American) interventions if necessary. [Theodore] Roosevelt justified such intervention as only an exercise of "police" power, but that term actually allowed United States presidents to intervene according to any criteria they were imaginative enough to devise. (LaFeber 1984, 38)

In the specific case of Haiti, U.S. president Woodrow Wilson justified its invasion and occupation on the ground that Haiti was in chaos following the overthrow and murder of Haitian president Vilbrun Guillaume Sam by angry mobs in July 1915 after he ordered some 167 political opponents to be killed and took refuge at the French Legation in Port-au-Prince. According to Wilson, the United States had an obligation to restore order and democracy to preserve the lives and property of American and other foreign citizens living in Haiti.

In testifying to the US Select Committee on Haiti and Santo Domingo on August 5, 1921, Stenio Vincent, then representing the Union Patriotique d'Haïti (and who would later become president of Haiti from 1930 to 1941), argued that notwithstanding the violent and tragic event that occurred on July 27, 1915, and resulted in the overthrow and death of President Sam,

> the life of not a single American or foreigner was taken or jeopardized. No property was destroyed. And although there was for the moment no government, there was no burning or killing or robbing. Quiet was promptly restored and a committee of public safety assumed responsibility for order until a new Government should be elected. It must be borne in mind that there was not a single instance of an American, or, indeed, of any foreigner having been killed or molested in Haiti prior to the American occupation. (Vincent 1921)

More to the point than reassuring the U.S. government that the lives and properties of United States and other foreign citizens were safe, Vincent pointed to the real reason for the U.S. invasion and occupation of Haiti: "The truth is that the Wilson administration took advantage of the political adventure of a weak and defenseless nation and forced upon it an intervention which, through the agency of the American minister in Haiti in December,

1914, of the Fort Smith mission in March, 1915, and of the Paul Fuller, Jr. mission in May, 1915, had been long in preparation" (Ibid.).

Indeed, well before the invasion in 1915, the U.S. government intervened on behalf of U.S. businesses in Haiti. It pressured the Haitian government to settle the claims of the MacDonald Company to pay the interests on the cost of constructing a railroad network in Haiti, to cede control over its customs receipts to the Banque Nationale, which had been taken over by U.S. financiers, and to sign a "satisfactory protocol" modeled on the American-Dominican Convention of 1907. The Wilson government decided to invade and occupy Haiti when it became clear that the Haitian government would not abide by these demands (Dupuy 1989, 31).

One of the first major acts of the occupying forces was to install the compliant government of Sudre Dartiguenave in August 1915 after compelling the members of the two chambers of the Haitian parliament (deputies and senators) to vote under the watchful eyes of the U.S. Marines. As Claude Moïse put it, "Dartiguenave's election represented a political accommodation and not a reestablishment of previous norms. The new head of state had no meaningful autonomy. Alongside the apparently legal government, the occupier progressively put in place its administrative apparatus comprised of civil and military functionaries" (Moïse 1990). As soon as this was done, the occupation authorities ordered Dartiguenave to sign the new Convention which henceforth granted the United States full control over Haiti's customs receipts, its finances, the public administration, health services, and public works, and replaced the old Haitian army with a new national police force. It became clear to all, then, that henceforth the Haitian "government and the political class could not entertain any illusion as to who was in charge" (Ibid.).

From the time the U.S. Marines landed in Haiti in July 1915 to the end of June 1920, the occupying forces confronted a continuous popular resistance, both armed and pacific, aimed at ending the occupation and returning control of the Haitian government to Haitians. As Suzy Castor put it, the resistance consisted of a political and anti-occupation narrative disseminated through various media comprised of nationalist sectors of the urban Haitian elite, and an armed resistance popularly known as the Cacos, who were comprised mostly of rural and peasant recruits. It was the latter that especially paid the price of resistance (Castor 1988, 128–155). But the suppression of the Cacos was also costly to its active members and other public supporters who collaborated with them. As Roger Gaillard summed it up, the victims of the war against the Cacos, those who succumbed to repression, from corvée labor, and from wounds and aftereffects of the war, some 15,000 Haitians lost their lives, a total "all the more impressive when compared to the 98 dead or wounded among the Marines and the Haitian and American gendarmes. That war, as in many other cases, is thus more akin to a massacre" (Gaillard 1983, 261–262).

While the occupying forces were suppressing the resistance, they were also creating the conditions for the investment of capital and the exploitation of Haitian labor and natural resources. To facilitate that process, the United States drafted and imposed a new constitution that for the first time since Haiti became independent allowed foreigners who were not married to Haitians to buy and own property. It created a centralized public administration, expanded technical education, and developed a modern infrastructure of roads and other transportation and communication networks to facilitate investments and the export of goods and raw materials to the United States. Though some U.S. businesses had been established in Haiti before 1915, many new ones followed on the heels of the occupation, including those involved in electricity, port and railroad construction, mining, banking, and large-scale plantation production such as pineapple, sisal, and sugar. Haitian banking and finance were placed under the control of U.S. banks, and the Haitian currency, the gourde, was henceforth pegged to the U.S. dollar rather than the French franc. And the United States became the single most important market for Haitian exports and imports (Dupuy 1989, 132–133).

For firms to be profitable and accumulate capital, however, they need a free wage-labor force, that is, people who, having no other means of subsistence at their disposal, are compelled to sell their labor-power (i.e., their ability to work rather than their whole person as happens in slavery) in order to live.[2] Prior to the occupation the vast majority of Haiti's working people, both men and women, were attached to the land and involved in subsistence agriculture and/or commercial activities, as in selling and buying goods in a market. Three categories of landed peasant farmers emerged during the nineteenth century: those who owned land and had legal titles; those who possessed land and were de facto but not de jure proprietors; and those who leased land through the métayage or sharecropping system from larger landowners. Those who owned/possessed land were also those who had larger, though still relatively small farms of approximately four to seven hectares (1 ha = 2.5 acres). Sharecroppers, on the other hand, leased their land from the landed bourgeoisie owning properties larger than 25 ha or 63 acres who subdivided their estates into smaller units. And below the categories of landowning/possessing peasants or sharecroppers were the landless peasants who hired themselves out as day laborers to those with land.

The transformation in the pattern of land ownership and the rise of a landed peasantry had significant effects on the relations between the dominant and subordinate classes. Because most of the rural population were farmers with access to land, they controlled the means and processes of production, and hence the rate of their exploitation. This was the case even where the landed bourgeoisie tried to extract more surplus from the sharecroppers. Unable to expropriate and transform most of the peasants with access to land and proletarianize them, the bourgeoisie was stymied in its efforts in the midnineteenth century to develop the national infrastructure in both the rural and urban areas, promote the growth of industries using agricultural and other raw materials for both domestic consumption and for export. Consequently, the dominant classes were limited to accumulating wealth primarily from the circulation rather than directly from the production process. They became a commercial and a rentier bourgeoisie that engaged in commercial and trade relations with other countries to which they could export Haitian agricultural products (principally coffee), and from which they could import durable and consumer goods they resold on the domestic market (Dupuy 1989, 85–95).

Among the first order of business for the occupation authorities was to expropriate the peasants from their land to create a wage-labor force that could be directly subsumed to and exploited by capital. From the outset that process had a dual aspect: creating a supply of labor for businesses operating in Haiti, and sending Haitian workers to other parts of the Caribbean such as the Dominican Republic and Cuba to work on American-owned sugar plantations. To supply the labor force for the businesses that came to Haiti, occupation and Haitian authorities evicted tens of thousands of peasant farmers from the lands they had occupied or leased from the government. And hundreds of thousands of hectares of land were transferred to foreign companies. The authorities adopted other measures to expropriate farmers, such as corvée labor, imposing taxes on alcohol that forced hundreds of small distilleries out of business, and not renewing leases or increasing the rents to farmers on state-owned lands. Agricultural companies, such as those producing sisal, bananas, and pineapple foreclosed the provision grounds of the farmers on their large estates, or as did the newly formed Haitian American Sugar Company, they contracted with small farmers to sell their crop to the company at very low prices, bankrupting them, and then hiring them as wage-laborers.

As Suzy Castor put it, "In fact, investments in agriculture and the establishment of plantations contributed to the appearance of an agricultural proletariat. Though relatively small and paid low wages, these workers represented a new element in the midst of the agrarian economy. Capitalist productions crystallized in paid labor were being implanted to a certain degree in the Haitian countryside" (Castor 1988, 97). In short, the occupation authorities and the Haitian governments they controlled used their power to proletarianize Haitian peasants. Just as force was used to land the Marines in and occupy Haiti, so it became how a Haitian proletariat was created. The Occupation accomplished in short order what the Haitian bourgeoisie had been unable to do for over 100 years (Dupuy 1989, 135–137).

II: 1934–1986: CLASS, COLOR, AND THE STRUGGLE FOR POWER AFTER THE OCCUPATION

Once unleashed, the proletarianization process continued unabated after the Occupation. In the 1930s, 1940s and 1950s, foreign companies came to Haiti to produce bananas, rubber, and to mine copper and bauxite for export. In 1942, the Lescot government granted the Haitian-American Agricultural Development Company a 50-year monopoly to produce and export rubber and expropriated over 133,000 hectares (328,643 acres) of land from peasant farmers in various parts of the country, amounting to about 21.5 percent of the cultivated area in Haiti. The company employed some 64,000 workers who were paid $0.30 for a 10-hour work day before it went bankrupt in 1945. Similarly, in 1944 the government granted a 60-year monopoly to the Reynolds Mining Corporation to extract and export bauxite by taking 375,000 hectares (926,625 acres) taken from thousands of local farmers. And in 1955, the government of Paul Magloire opened the country to copper mining by granting a contract to the Canadian company, International Halliwell Mines Limited (Brisson 1976, 77–89). As could be expected, and as was the case with the foreign, mainly United States, companies that came to Haiti during the Occupation, so it was that the profits of these extractive industries were not reinvested in Haiti but transferred to their headquarters in the United States or Canada.

These standard practices of foreign capital notwithstanding, Guy Pierre pointed out, the successive Haitian governments could have pursued policies to encourage and promote a more coherent development strategy during the 25 years that the extractive industries operated in Haiti. None of that happened, he concluded, because the Haitian state was not only too weak, but its leaders were too disorganized, too incoherent, and too corrupt to coordinate such a long-term development strategy. All this led to the conclusion that under such a "climate of outright robbery and sinecure that prevailed during these years at the center of the power structure—an important part of the flow of capital disappeared each year without leaving any traces behind in the national budget" (Pierre 2017, 145). Those practices have not changed. Since its inception as an independent country, the state has been a site for the promotion and enrichment of the factions of the middle and dominant classes that controlled it, and which Robert Fatton aptly calls "la politique du ventre (politics of the belly)" (Fatton 2014, 25).

The proletarianization of Haitian peasants was not limited to supplying a labor force for the businesses operating in Haiti only. During the Occupation tens of thousands of Haitian workers went to work on U.S-owned sugar and other agricultural plantations in Cuba and the Dominican Republic. But whereas Haitian migration to Cuba ended in 1937 and tens of thousands were deported to Haiti in 1938, it continues unabated, not only to the Dominican Republic even after the massacre of some ten to twenty-five thousand Haitians by the Trujillo government in 1937, but to other parts of the Caribbean, South America, North America, especially the United States and Canada, and France.

The Occupation also transformed the class structure and balance of power in Haiti in ways other than the proletarianization of the peasantry. The most important was the rise of a small but significant urban middle class of professionals and white-collar workers spawned by both the expansions of job opportunities in the private sector and the growth of a civil bureaucracy and state institutions (e.g., in education, public works, sanitation, and health), in addition to the new Haitian army and police.

Mulattoes and blacks belonged to the middle class and the lower stratum of the bourgeoisie, but blacks predominated in both and were intensely conscious of the correlation between skin color and upward social mobility. During the Occupation, mulattoes, favored by the Occupation authorities, were placed in key positions in the government and the various state apparatuses, including the military. During and briefly after the Occupation, mulattoes also gained control of the presidency, such as those of Louis Borno (1922–1930), Sténio Vincent (1930–1941), and Élie Lescot (1941–1946), and they directly challenged the black middle class's traditional means of social ascension, thereby elevating the "color question" to the center stage ideologically and politically. The struggle between those two factions reached a decisive turning point in 1946 when the black-nationalist forces succeeded in electing Dumarsais Estimé as president.[3] His presidency was short-lived, but it allowed the black middle class, in alliance with the provincial and urban black bourgeoisie, to regain its dominance in the government and public administration. But it was in 1957 that the black-nationalist forces reached their apogee with the election of François Duvalier,[4] which he soon transformed into a 29 year dictatorship by transferring power in 1971 to his son Jean-Claude before he died. The son ruled until he was overthrown and exiled in February 1986.

Three essential aspects of the Duvalier regime were consequential for future political and economic developments. First, the principal objective of the regime under François Duvalier was not to alter the class structure of Haiti and hence the economic dominance of the predominantly mulatto bourgeoisie,[5] but to recapture political power for the black bourgeoisie and middle class. It achieved this by purging most, but not all, mulattoes from the top positions in the government, public administration, and the military. And, never fully trusting the military even after having chosen officers to run it, the regime created a parallel military force to the Haitian army called the Volunteers for National Security (popularly known as the Tontons Macoutes) that Duvalier controlled directly, and which was used as the regime's security and terror apparatus. Once in place, the state unleashed a reign of terror unprecedented in Haiti's history. Going beyond the repressiveness of previous dictatorships, the regime spared no one from its violence. Men, women, children, families from all classes, and even entire towns were subject to the regime's ruthless and unpredictable terror.

No major state and civil society institutions were left untouched or allowed to function independently: the legislature, judiciary, and civil administration were all brought under the direct control of Duvalier, and the regime suppressed all hitherto independent political, trade union, media, and other civil society organizations by arresting, killing, or exiling their leaders who were considered a threat to the regime. Even the Catholic Church came under the regime's control when Duvalier expelled all foreign clergy and replaced them with Haitians. As Michel-Rolph Trouillot observed succinctly, Duvalier "did not seek the physical intervention of the State in the battlefield of politics; it aimed to create a void in that field to the benefit of the State. It wanted an end to that struggle for a lack of combatants in the sphere occupied by the totalitarian executive" (1986, 180).

The cost of capturing and consolidating power for the black-nationalist faction of the bourgeoisie and middle class, therefore, was quite high. In addition to the tens of thousands of citizens killed by the regime, the economy and the standard of living of most of the population deteriorated; and the regime alienated the mulatto bourgeoisie as well as the United States and other western European powers, which suspended direct military and financial aid but made no effort to topple it. The economic isolation of the regime compelled it to adopt a second strategy, namely, to attract new foreign investments and financial and military aid by offering significant advantages to foreign investors such as tax exemptions, an abundance of cheap labor, and a climate of labor peace by suppressing all independent labor organizations and banning strikes.

These measures led U.S. president Richard Nixon to resume full financial and military aid in 1969. But that did not lead to the renewal of foreign investments immediately. It was not until after Jean-Claude Duvalier assumed power in 1971 that foreign businesses began to do so. This third aspect of the regime was characterized by what I called a triple alliance among the Duvalier regime, the black and mulatto bourgeoisie, and foreign capital, with the first two components as junior partners (Dupuy 2007, 42–44). Essentially the Haitian government turned over the formulation of economic policy to the United States and the IFIs, the World Bank, the International Monetary Fund, and the Inter-American Development Bank whose policies are largely dictated by the United States.

Capitalizing on Haiti's poverty, a climate of labor peace achieved through brutal repression, and an abundant and unskilled labor force, these institutions pushed the Haitian government to adopt and implement a set of neoliberal policies—reductions on tariff and trade restrictions, tax incentives to investors, privatization of public enterprises, reduction of public spending and public sector employees—that would ultimately transform Haiti into a supplier of the cheapest labor in the Western Hemisphere for the export assembly manufacturing industries, and from being nearly self-sufficient into a net importer of foods from the United States, rice in particular. Rather than generating sustainable economic development, these policies exacerbated poverty and income and wealth inequalities, and spurred more emigration.

Even if it was not as brutally repressive as the father's, the son's regime could not reform itself sufficiently to accommodate the popular demand for democratic reforms and civil and human rights that emerged in the early 1980s. This movement was not only the first major wave of political opposition to emerge since the U.S. Occupation in the provinces before it spread to the capital city of Port-au-Prince. As Claude Moïse and Émile Olivier pointed out, that movement signaled that the Duvalier regime no longer monopolized the political discourse and that the people were beginning to reflect aloud about the country's problems and their solutions (1992, 70–72). Even the Catholic Church was compelled to criticize the regime's corruption and repression of dissidents, thereby further weakening it, and legitimizing the popular opposition.

As that movement grew and became more radical, the United States was faced with two alternatives: continue to back the discredited Duvalier regime and risk the further radicalization of the popular movement and increasing anti-U.S. sentiments or abandon the regime and save itself from having to intervene militarily. The United States chose the second alternative, compelled Duvalier to leave Haiti and turned to the military to contain the opposition with the promise of democratic elections (Dupuy 1997, 49–50). Jean-Claude Duvalier left Haiti in 1986 and went into exile in France. Michel-Rolph Trouillot offered a succinct summary of the role of the United States in Duvalier's ouster:

> Duvalier's departure and the constitution of the CNG (Conseil National de Gouvernement) was a multinational exercise in "crisis management," a calculated break in the democratic path that the Haitian people had embarked

upon. We may never learn the details of the negotiations [that led to Duvalier's departure], but negotiations there were. And we need not know these details, or fully investigate ex-Marine Colonel Oliver North's claim to have brought an end to Haiti's nightmare, to be certain of one crucial fact: Jean-Claude Duvalier was brought down by a high-level coup d'état executed with international connivance. (1990, 226)

Essentially, the CNG indeed resulted from a connivance concocted by the fallen dictator, the military, the United States, Canada, France, and the hierarchy of the Catholic Church to find a compromise that could appease the Duvalierists who wanted to remain in power and the broad democratic opposition that was demanding nothing less than a complete uprooting of the Duvalierists and the creation of a democratic government that would for the first time represent the interests of the majority rather than those of the dominant classes and their foreign overlords. For the next four years, amidst continuing human rights violations by the military and five successive and short-lived governments—three headed by military generals and two by civilians—the broad but determined forces of the opposition finally led to the creation of a Council of State to organize presidential elections in December 1990 governed by the new 1987 Constitution. Jean-Bertrand Aristide, then a fiery Liberation Theology priest, won that election by a landslide (Dupuy 1989, 47–68).

III: DEMOCRACY FOR WHOM? THE THIRD PHASE OF TRANSFORMATION: 1991–2016

When Aristide assumed the presidency in February 1991, he sought to implement what he called a "growth with equity" or "basic needs" model aimed at protecting domestic food production, especially rice, against cheaper imports, raising the minimum wage of workers in the assembly industries, increasing revenues by taxing profits, tariffs, and patents on the principle of equity, eliminating favoritism to the wealthy, and combatting corruption and curbing waste in public spending (Ibid.). As moderate as it was, that reform program ran afoul of the interests of the Haitian business class, the military, the IFIs, and the United States. The Haitian army, whose disbanding he had called for, toppled Aristide in September 1991. The message that was being sent to Aristide and his supporters was that the concept of rule of the people, by the people, and for the people, was incompatible with the rule of capital. As Ellen Meiksins Wood put it, in such a system, the economic sphere becomes invulnerable to democratic power:

> Preserving that invulnerability has even become an essential criterion of democracy. This definition allows us to invoke democracy against the empowerment of people in the economic sphere. It even makes it possible to invoke democracy in defense of a curtailment of democratic rights in other parts of "civil society" or even in the political domain, if that is what is needed to protect property and the market against democratic power. (Wood 1995, 235)

For the Haitian ruling class and the major powers and their institutions that devised policies for Haiti, the line between what I have called a minimalist democracy and a maximalist democracy was never to be crossed. By the former, I mean a democratic order in which markets are minimally regulated and where basic rights are limited to the usual freedom of speech, a free press, the right to assemble, to own property, and to participate in elections and form political parties to contest them. This is in keeping with the expectations of the United States and the IFIs who devised policy for Haiti. By contrast, I mean by a maximalist democracy that all citizens must be guaranteed not only the basic rights mentioned above, but the right to economic security that would require a curb on the prerogatives of private capital and a more equal distribution of wealth and income in addition to free access to education, health care, transportation, and adequate housing. Even if Aristide and his Operation Lavalas organization had not fully embraced the latter version of democracy, it was clear that the combined demands of the broad popular movement for democracy that propelled him to office were more in line with the maximalist than the minimalist version of democracy outlined above (Dupuy 2007, 18–19).

For his part, and notwithstanding all his rhetoric against the IFI like the IMF which he once referred to as the "International Misery Front," Aristide was open to concessions before his overthrow, such as, for example, when he signed a Stand-by agreement with the IMF in September 1991 shortly before he was overthrown (Ibid.). But whatever qualms he may have had about accepting the neoliberal policies when he became president, all that had changed during his three years in exile. When President Clinton returned Aristide to Haiti in October 1994 on the back of 20,000 U.S. Marines to complete the 18 months left in his five-year term, he agreed to lower tariffs on rice and other food imports to 3 percent (Chavla 2010; Katz 2013). They have remained at that level since.

These policies had drastic consequences for the agricultural sector and for Haitian farmers. Whereas in the 1970s Haiti imported about 19 percent of its food needs, currently it imports 35 percent. It went from being self-sufficient in the production of rice, sugar, poultry, and pork to becoming the fourth-largest importer of subsidized U.S. rice in the world and the largest importer of foodstuffs from the United States in the Caribbean. Eighty percent of all the rice consumed in Haiti is now imported. Trade liberalization, then, essentially meant transferring wealth from Haitian to U.S. farmers, especially rice farmers in Arkansas and the U.S. agribusiness companies that export to Haiti and those Haitian firms that resell it on the domestic market. Not surprisingly, rice imports topped the list in terms of profitability (McGuigan 2006; Dupuy 2014, 123). As former U.S. president Clinton acknowledged, since 1981 the United States has been pursuing a policy of selling food to poor countries "to relieve them of the burden of producing their own food so they can leap directly into the industrial era. It has not worked. It may have been good for some of my farmers in Arkansas, but it has not worked. It was a mistake I was party to. I am not pointing a finger at anybody. I did that. I have to live every day with the consequences of the lost capacity to produce a rice crop in Haiti to feed those people because of what I did" (Ibid.).

In short, the development strategies devised by Washington and the IFIs that they imposed on Haiti exacerbated its underdevelopment and worsened the disparities between the wealthy elites and the subordinated classes. Along with Bolivia, Haiti has the largest income inequality in the hemisphere. In 1976, 75 percent of the population lived in conditions of absolute poverty, and about 5 percent of the population appropriated more than 50 percent of the national income. By 2007, the richest 10 percent of the population appropriated 47 percent of national income, and 2 percent controlled 26 percent of the nation's wealth. By contrast, the poorest 20 percent received 1.1 percent of national income; 76 percent of the population lived on less than U.S.$2/day, and more than half lived on less than U.S.$1/day (Inter-American Development Bank 2007).

When Aristide won reelection for a second and final five-year term in November 2000, the balance of class forces had shifted even more in favor of the bourgeoisie and the organized political opposition against him. In the absence of a strong popular movement to pressure him, Aristide sought an accommodation with the bourgeoisie and foreign capital by implementing the recommended neoliberal policies of privatizing public enterprises and reducing tariffs to their lowest levels as I mentioned above. He also negotiated a deal with the World Bank and the Inter-American Development Bank to create a free-trade zone in northern Haiti that required the expropriation of farmers and the appropriation of more than a thousand acres of farmland in the region. But none of these measures won him the support of the international community, especially the United States under the George W. Bush administration, the Haitian bourgeoisie, or his political opponents. In addition to their intense dislike and distrust of Aristide, the political opposition especially feared that given his control of both houses of the legislature, Aristide would amend the 1987 Constitution to remove the restriction on two consecutive presidential terms and prolong his power indefinitely. For them, then, the only solution was to remove Aristide from power. Fully backed by the United States, France, and Canada, the Haitian bourgeoisie and the opposition coalition did exactly that in 2004—and again exiled him to South Africa until he returned to Haiti in 2011 (Dupuy 2007, esp. Ch 6; 2011).

An interim government installed by the international community succeeded Aristide and was supported by a United Nations peacekeeping force whose main task was to pacify the country and neutralize the remnants of Aristide's more militant and sometimes armed supporters. René Préval was then reelected for a second and final term in 2006. The United Nations Mission to Haiti (MINUSTAH as it was known by its French acronym) did not leave the country until mid-October 2017.

In January 2010, a massive earthquake struck Haiti and killed more than 200,000 people, injured more than 300,000, destroyed more than 250,000 commercial, industrial, administrative, and residential buildings, and displaced more than 1.5 million people. The estimated value of the damage ranged from between $7 and 14 billion. The international community, with the United States, Canada, France, and the United Nations in the leading roles, responded quickly and swiftly with some 39 countries and people from countries around the world sending money and emergency aid of various sort: doctors, nurses, food, medicine, water, temporary shelters, portable hospitals, communication, and heavy equipment to help remove the rubble.

Under the leadership of the United States, an Interim Haiti Reconstruction Commission (IHRC) was created and comprised representatives from 26 countries, including Haiti, and co-chaired by former U.S. president Bill Clinton and Haitian prime minister Jean-Max Bellerive that set forth an Action Plan for the Reconstruction and National Development of Haiti. It became clear at the outset that the IHRC had displaced the Haitian government and equally ignored the voices and priorities of various cross-sections of Haitian society in setting up its plan of action, a fact that Prime Minister Bellerive admitted openly (Dupuy 2010, 15). As Robert Fatton put it so clearly, "Haitians are not really in charge of their own affairs; it is the dominant international financial institutions, that have elaborated the country's economic plans for development. Powerful domestic and international interests constrain presidential leadership into embracing old strategies and reflexes. The government is at best weak, and at worst an empty shell" (Fatton 2014, 98).

Essentially, and not surprisingly, the IHRC proposed the same neo-liberal policies for Haiti's post-earthquake development strategy that had so miserably failed to deliver their promise before, and which Clinton himself had decried, as already noted. This time, the IHRC adopted a set of policies laid out in a report commissioned by the United Nations from Paul Collier, a former World Bank economist (and Oxford University professor), before the 2010 earthquake that laid out the same strategies the United States and the IFIs had advocated since the 1970s: attracting assembly manufacturing industries to Haiti due to its low-wages, removing barriers to free trade and privatizing public enterprises, and curbing social spending to reduce fiscal deficits (Collier 2009).

As could be expected, the policies recommended by the IHRC failed to generate any more meaningful post-earthquake economic development than those adopted before. They were not meant to. As before, their primary objective was to make it possible for foreign investors in Haiti and their domestic business partners to profit from Haiti's low-wage labor force and to open Haiti's market to foreign imports of food and other commodities by lowering tariffs. As I will show more fully in the next chapter, the labor force employed in the assembly manufactures in Haiti is primarily female because, given the gender division of labor and the suppression and discrimination women face, they are paid on average 32 percent less than male workers, ceteris paribus (Singh and Barton-Dock 2015, 35). In a country like Haiti with consistently high rates of unemployment, and with most workers earning less than the minimum wage, employers have little difficulty finding and hiring workers willing to accept low wages in the assembly industry (and other sectors of the formal economy). As a Haitian owner/contractor of one of the largest garment industries put it, "When you have a country where 80 percent [sic] (Marcus 2019, 4)[6] of the population don't work, anything is good!" Another justified the low wages of workers thusly: "If you don't work, you don't have anything. With the wages they get at least they can survive. It's better than nothing" (Ayti Kale Je 2011).

The conditions for the majority have not improved significantly since the earthquake, although extreme poverty declined from 31 percent in 2000 to 24 percent in 2012 with most of the improvement occurring in urban areas. In 2018, nearly 60 percent of the population was living under the national poverty level, and 24 percent were considered extreme poor. More than half of the population were unable to meet their basic needs, and 2.5 million unable to cover their food needs. At the other end of the scale, the wealthiest 10 percent of the population appropriated nearly 50 percent of the national income while the lowest 10 percent received 0.7 percent. And the top 1 percent of the population had 50 times more resources at its disposal than the bottom 10 percent, making Haiti one of the most unequal countries in the world in terms of income and wealth distribution (Central Intelligence Agency 2019; Singh and Barton-Dock 2015, 29).

NOTES

1. Originally published in French in *Haitian History Journal*, No. 2 (2021): 125–156. Reprinted with permission.

2. Slave labor, as I have argued elsewhere, was also quite profitable at the time of capitalism's emergence as a world system. But that alternative was no longer available in Haiti since the revolution of 1791–1804 (Knight and Martinez-Vergne 2019, esp. Ch. 1).

3. Until 1957, Haitian presidents were elected indirectly by the legislature, which itself was elected by popular vote. Such elections were meaningless, however, since the coup d'état was the primary means of creating and undoing governments during the nineteenth and twentieth centuries.

4. Contrary to most accounts, the first universal election in Haiti—where both men and women could vote—was in 1957, not 1990 when Jean-Bertrand Aristide was elected president. Despite a heavy military presence during the election and its support for Duvalier, he in fact won the popular vote (see Trouillot, 1986, 160-167; Dupuy, 1989, 155-157).

5. When I speak of the Haitian bourgeoisie, both mulatto and black, as it evolved during the twentieth century, I am referring to the 1 to 2 percent of the population, including members of the Levantine immigrants who came to Haiti early in the twentieth century, many of whom and their descendants married Haitians. The economic base of this class consisted of import/export firms, manufacturing industries, often in partnership with foreign investors, large land holders, those who occupied high public office they used as a mean of enrichment, and professionals (especially those in the medical and legal professions who originated from that class).

6. Some estimates put the unemployment rate at 60 percent.

3

The Political Economy of Class and Gender in Haiti

This chapter has four parts. Part I offers an assessment and critique of the argument, originally advanced by Mireille Neptune Anglade, that in Haiti women labor for the benefit and the enrichment of men in general. I argue instead that the oppression and exploitation of women are best understood in the context of the class relations and divisions of labor in Haiti and its position and function in the capitalist world economy. Part II draws on the work of other theorists to develop a Marxist perspective on gender and class relations in contemporary capitalism. Part III applies that perspective to analyze the specific modes of gender divisions and exploitation in the context of the class and power relations of Haiti. Part IV summarizes this argument and points to the way forward to transforming the unequal gender and class relations and constructing a democratic socialist society in Haiti.

I

In *L'autre moitié du développement: à propos du travail des femmes en Haïti* (1986), Mireille Neptune Anglade offers an incisive analysis of the gender division of labor and its consequences for women in Haiti. She concludes that "the female, by paying the price for all the degradation of the national whole and by assuming an important invisible work, in fact ensures the transfer of the resources of life and survival to the MASCULINE" (Anglade 1986, 14, emphasis in the original).

Anglade recognizes that Haiti is also characterized by class divisions and that the dominant and capitalist classes are quite wealthy by exploiting the labor of the subordinate classes. Nonetheless, she maintains, the transfer of wealth from women's labor to men can be measured globally in general terms that make men the beneficiaries of the exploitation of women, but also in terms of the number of hours worked, of supplementary income, more leisure time, greater prestige, more availability for wage labor, and more social and economic opportunities (Ibid.).

The strength of Anglade's study is that she grounds the causes and consequences of the exploitation and degradation of women firmly in the social relations and structures of the division of labor of Haiti's economy rather than in their ideological and cultural manifestations and justifications, but without ignoring the latter. She evokes Simone de Beauvoir's famous dictum that "One is not born, but rather becomes a woman" (de Beauvoir 1974, 301; Anglade 1986, 215), and follows that with Andrée Michel's remark that likewise "one is not born a man, but becomes one" (Michel 1985, 4–8). Anglade makes it clear that these ideological formulations are the expressions of, and justifications for, the subordination and exploitation of women rather than their cause. As de Beauvoir put it, "no biological, psychological, or economic fate determines the figure that the human female presents in society; it is civilization as a whole that produces this creature. Only the intervention of someone else can establish an individual as an Other" (de Beauvoir 1974, 302).

A useful analogy could be made here with the role that ideological discourses played in the production of difference and the processes of "Othering," such as was the case with "race" and racialization. In a vein similar to de Beauvoir's, Stuart Hall argued that "race" cannot offer the proof or fix the meaning of cultural difference that either those who support or oppose racial oppression would like it to because the "chain of equivalences that race makes possible between genetic, physical, social, and cultural differences does not actually exist," despite the fact that it is used pervasively to make sense of social life and the social practices we engage into. This is what gives "race" its reality "because it has racial effects—material effects in how power and resources are distributed, symbolic effects in how groups are ranked relationally to one another, psychic effects that form the interior space of existence of every subject constructed by it and caught up in the play of its signifiers." Hall goes on to argue that sexual difference is also used to "read the evidence of the body discursively, trying to fix social and cultural meanings biologically, and thereby acquiring something of the same pervasive obviousness as race" (Hall 2017, 69, 70).

For Teresa Ebert, social differences are both maintained and contested ideologically as they respond to social realities and contradictions generated by the social divisions of labor, and are solved ideologically in the cultural imaginary by naturalizing those differences. It is through ideology that practices and subjectivities are situated in specific social differences and those relations are naturalized as inevitable. From this it follows that insofar as the exploitation and extraction of surplus labor from women are objective realities in class societies, transformative politics requires changing those social relations (Ebert 1999, 8, 38).

I agree with Anglade's and others like Carolle Charles's (1995, 142) depictions of the gender division of labor and the subordination of, oppression, discrimination, and exploitation in all dimensions in Haiti. But I disagree with their contention that women labor for the welfare and enrichment of men in general regardless of their class position. By so arguing they reduce the divisions in Haitian society as being between men and women of all classes rather than between the dominant and subordinate classes and the divisions of labor on which they are predicated. It follows that for them the solution for these conditions is not to transform the class structures and relations of production and exploitation in Haiti, wherein both men and women in the dominant classes exploit the labor and extract surplus value (profit) and wealth from men and women in the working and peasant classes. It is, rather, to equalize the conditions of women vis-à-vis those of men.

Among other measures, Anglade argues, the reforms should aim at making it possible for women to have access to health care and social services, implementing social and judicial reforms to protect women and children, making men equally responsible for the care and education of their children, implementing an agrarian reform to allow women to have access to property to reduce the necessity for them to emigrate to urban areas, improving their working conditions in industry and regulating and increasing their salaries accordingly, making more services available to children, and ensuring that women have full and equal rights (Anglade 1986, 220).

Leaving aside that most men in Haiti are poor; do not have equal access to property, education, or health care; and are compelled to migrate to urban areas or emigrate to find employment, as are poor women, Anglade's recommendations are worth fighting for in one of the most unequal countries in the world in terms of income and wealth distribution, access to life's necessities, and a decent living worthy of human dignity. In the end, however, such reforms would not transform the class structures or the divisions of labor in Haiti or end the exploitation of women. They would instead make women in the subordinate and working classes as equally exploited as men in those classes are.

To help clarify this point, it is important to understand the difference between "benefiting" and "profiting" from or being "enriched" by someone else's labor, and between income and wealth.[1] Working class men, for example, may well benefit from women's labor, such as the unpaid labor they perform in the home that gives men more leisure time, greater availability for wage labor, more prestige, and more opportunities to pursue other goals, as Anglade pointed out. They also benefit from the discrimination against women in the labor market insofar as men are paid more than women for doing the same work, ceteris paribus. But no matter how much they earn from their labor, they are exploited by and remain at the mercy of their employers if they don't continue to generate profits, that is, wealth, for the owners of the firms.

Nancy Fraser makes this clear by distinguishing between what she calls redistributive and transformative justice. A class is first and foremost rooted in the economic structure of society and exists as a collective body only by virtue of its position in that structure and its relation to other social classes. In a capitalist society, the working class comprises the individual men and women who are compelled to sell their labor power to the capitalist class under conditions and arrangements created and controlled by the latter who appropriate the surplus value (profits) the workers generate.

From this it follows that while the capitalist classes appropriate wealth in the form of profits from the labor of men and women in the working classes, incomes are distributed unequally among the working classes, not only because of the different qualifications (such as education and skills) they bring to the market, but also from discrimination and other cultural injustices that women and men are subjected to. Rather than being "rooted directly in an autonomously unjust cultural structure, these derive from political economy, as ideologies of class inferiority proliferate to justify exploitation. The remedy for the injustice, consequently, is the recognition of the devalued and discriminated-against groups. Overcoming class exploitation, on the other hand, requires restructuring the political economy so as to alter the class distribution of social burdens and social benefits" (Fraser 1997, 18).

For those collectivities like women who suffer both cultural and economic injustice, then, the remedy is both recognition and redistribution because gender structures the division between paid "productive" labor and unpaid "reproductive" and domestic labor to which women are primarily assigned. Gender also structures the unequal distribution of wages and salaries between men and women, with the former receiving more than the latter for equivalent work, ceteris paribus. This kind of injustice, therefore, calls for redistributive remedies and it is essentially Anglade's position. However, Fraser goes on, much like class, gender is a political–economic differentiation endowed with certain class-like characteristics, and it calls for both redistributive measures and the transformation of the political economy: "The logic of the remedy is akin to the logic with respect to class: it is to put gender out of business as such" (Ibid., 19).

II: TOWARD AN ALTERNATIVE PARADIGM: CAPITAL, CLASS, AND GENDER

Capitalism is a social system of commodity production for sale in a market for profit. The social actors required for that system are, on the one hand, an individual in possession of money and seeking to invest it to produce commodities and sell them in a market, and whose values (expressed in the form of market prices) are higher than the costs of producing them (i.e., a profit) and, on the other hand, an individual who, having no independent means of producing/providing for his or her needs (like peasants who own and/or possess their own land, produce and consume their own food, and sell what they don't consume in a market), is thereby compelled to offer his or her labor power to the owner of the means of production in return for a salary. In that sense, then, all capital, embodied in the owner of money and means of production, needs is not any specific seller of labor power clothed in any descriptive category such as white, black, brown, man, woman, lesbian, gay, bisexual, transgender (LGBT), adult, or child. It just needs to be able to find those whose only means of survival is to sell their labor power "freely"[2] to the owner of capital in a labor market and produce commodities or services at a profit for the employer or business owner (Harvey 2014, 7–8; Dupuy 2014, 7–32).

As they developed globally since the sixteenth century, capitalist relations of production and divisions of labor never conformed to the abstract formulations of the personae representing the capitalist and the laborer meeting in a nondescript market to exchange the production of commodities and create profits for the former and wages for the latter. In the different regions/countries where they took root initially (England, Western Europe) or that were forcefully incorporated in this global system via imperialist/colonial conquests (the New World, Asia, India, Africa) these capitalist relations and divisions of labor wore different clothing and labels, such as owners of capital and the laborers they employed, including men, women, and children whether they were white, black, or brown, and who were hierarchized accordingly depending on the positions they occupied in the production process and the relative power relations among those social actors at different times and places.

There are important differences in the specific historical origins of the ideologies of race and gender and the role they played in the division of labor in modern capitalism since the sixteenth century. There had been attempts to distinguish and categorize people of different religions (e.g., Christians, Moors, and Jews) during the Spanish Inquisition in the late fifteenth and early sixteenth centuries to justify the right to rule by the "true and pure" members of the nobility. But these demarcations never produced ideologies of "race" as such. The idea of "purity of blood" subsequently led to the "mark of race" for those who were not initially distinguished because of their skin color (Hannaford 1996, 122–126; Davis 2006, 79). The transition to the "mark of race" occurred with the European colonization of the Americas in the sixteenth century, the capture of Africans and their transplantation to the colonies to create the system of chattel slavery to supply the labor force for the plantation economy.

The creation of a racialized labor force in the New World based on the exploitation of African slaves and laborers imported from Western Europe and England led to the development of racial/ethnic categories and their concomitant ideologies of racism to rationalize their unequal rankings and allocation to different positions in the division of labor since the seventeenth century. For racism to take hold in one's imaginary, be seen as "natural," and invoke feelings of antipathy and of cultural superiority or inferiority, it needs to be based on visible and unchangeable markers of difference that must be maintained and reproduced generationally through social and spatial distancing to avoid the possibility of blurring the lines of difference over time.

This is what W. E. B. Dubois called the "color line" (Dubois 1969, 54, 198, and passim), which made it possible for those who came to be classified as "white" or as "black" to internalize these differences and act accordingly to maintain what social advantage one could gain over the other in the labor market and the society at large. David Roediger, for example, showed how the Irish immigrants who came to the United States before the Civil War faced intense animosity from native-born whites who often compared them to blacks. To gain acceptance into the "white race," they quickly embraced the same racist attitudes toward blacks so they could benefit from "the particular 'public and psychological wages' whiteness offered to a desperate rural and often preindustrial Irish population coming to labor in industrializing American cities" (Roediger 1991, 137). Similarly, Mary Waters argued, other white immigrants who also faced discrimination, such as the Irish, eventually assimilated into the broad mainstream of white society while exercising their "ethnic options" or "symbolic ethnicity" that allowed them to choose to identify as Irish, English, or German without being questioned or thought of as "passing" as other than whom they claimed to be (Waters 1990, 18–19).

Black Africans, however, were not allowed to exercise such options, even though, as with white European immigrants, they were not homogeneous and came from different parts of Africa; had different cultures, skin complexions, and hair textures; and spoke different languages (Thornton 1988, 183). But, unlike white immigrants they were "constrained to identify as blacks even when they believed or knew that their forebears included many non-blacks" (Ibid.). As Barbara Fields observed poignantly, "race is not an element of human biology, nor is it an idea that can be plausibly imagined to live an eternal life of its own. Race is not an idea but an ideology. It came into existence at a discernible historical moment for rationally understandable historical reasons and is subject to change for similar reasons" (Fields 1990, 101).

If there is a direct link between the rise of modern capitalism and the invention of the concepts of "race" and "ethnicity" predicated on the differential valuation and rankings of the human population based on perceived phenotypical differences to justify the stratification of the workforce globally as well as within specific nation-states, the same cannot be said of gender and its attendant ideologies. Gender relations and divisions predated modern capitalism by centuries, having had their origin historically in Ancient Greece during the transition from the matriarchal family structure, where descent was traced along the female line and property remained within her gens, to patriarchy. Frederick Engels describes the transition to patriarchy as the "overthrow of mother right," and with it the "world historical defeat of the female sex." Once that happened, the man henceforth took control of the household and of inheritance, and "the woman was degraded and reduced to servitude; she became the slave of his lust and a mere instrument for the production of children. The degraded position of the woman, especially conspicuous among the Greeks of the heroic and still more of the classical age, has gradually been palliated and glossed over, and sometimes clothed in a milder form; in no sense has it been abolished" (Engels 1973, 121).

Indeed, the patriarchal household and the nuclear family continue to play a key role in the reproduction of the class structures of capitalism and the men and women that comprise them, even if other forms, such as single-parent or same-sex households, have emerged. As Martha Gimenez pointed out, while in a capitalist society the different biological roles of men and women must be preserved, there is a key difference between the reproductive roles of the capitalist and working-class families. The men and women of the capitalist class do not have to sell their labor power to survive if they ensure the generational reproduction of the members of that class and the preservation of their property. By contrast the men and women of the working classes must sell their labor power to the capitalist classes to survive, and they also reproduce themselves as such and thereby continue to supply future members of that class for capital. It is therefore essential to retain and reproduce members of the respective classes "through superstructural conditions (legal, ethical, religious, ideological) that universalize it for all classes, obscuring the qualitative differences between classes in the process of defining everyone as a legal, political, ethical subject" (Gimenez 1997, 16).

It is at this juncture that ideology plays its central role in justifying the differences between men and women—as it did for the distinctions between "white" and "black"—that express themselves ideologically and materially in all spheres of social life and are also contested. Ideology, Teresa Ebert suggests, "responds to the contradictory social reality that is the outcome of the division of labor, which restricts access to social and economic resources through class. Material contradictions produced in the economic practices of capitalism are "solved" ideologically in the cultural imaginary by naturalizing social differences" (Ebert 1999, 8).

As Elizabeth Corredor pointed out also, the gains the feminist and LGBTQ+ movement made in the early 1990s led the Vatican to attack what it considered the "'misleading concepts concerning sexuality and the dignity and mission of women" that led to a "'misunderstanding of the complementary difference between man and woman," and "a growing confusion about sexual identity" that "complicates the assumption of roles and the sharing of tasks in the home.'" For the Catholic Church, then, gender ideologies that deny that the differences between men and women are not fixed in nature but are produced culturally are disruptive because they promote homosexuality and create gender confusion (Corredor 2019, 615).

Given their ownership of and control over the means of production and reproduction, Ebert argues, bourgeois women in capitalist households—and, I would add, in those of the highly paid middle-class professionals and office holders—are freed from the routine and menial dimensions of reproduction and partially from social reproduction. They delegate such tasks as housework, childcare, and some aspects of child socialization to paid domestic workers, most of whom are women (Ibid.).

In working-class households, by contrast, the domestic labor performed by women is essential for the survival and well-being of all its members. As Rosa Luxemburg noted, household labor is not considered productive in the sense of the present capitalist economy no matter the energy spent or sacrifices made because such labor does not produce surplus value or profit for the capitalist (Luxemburg 1971, 221).[3]

Insofar as members of working-class families depend on the sale of their labor power to earn their wages and have traditionally relied on the domestic labor of women to reproduce their labor power, caring for the children and the sick, and performing other household tasks, this puts men in the household in a position to become the principal wage earners and exercise greater power over women, whether they are also employed outside the home. Domestic labor, then, provides necessary services to the working class, is an important component in the reproduction of its labor power on both a daily and generational basis, and benefits the capitalist class by cheapening the overall level of wages while increasing the surplus value (profits) they can extract from those who work (Gimenez 1997, 79).

At the same time, the division between unpaid domestic labor and paid wage labor for those who work outside the home puts men and women in a competitive and antagonistic relation toward each other. Those who are wage earners are in a relative position of power over those who are primarily unpaid domestic workers, thereby turning domestic labor into a structural alternative to wage labor. Engels brought that relationship into sharp focus by remarking that when the woman in a family is employed and her husband is not, the relations between them are reversed. The man becomes "unsexed" and takes away the "womanliness of the woman without being able to bestow upon the man true womanliness, or the woman true manliness." Consequently,

> we must either despair of mankind, and its aims and efforts, when we see all our labor and toil result in such a mockery, or we must admit that human society has hitherto sought salvation in a false direction; if the reign of the wife over the husband, as inevitably brought about by the factory system, is inhuman, the pristine rule of the husband over the wife must have been inhuman too. (Engels 1975, 439)

Gender inequalities and the discrimination women are subjected to when they perform unpaid domestic labor do more than put them in a subordinate and dependent relation in the household when men are the primary or principal wage earners. These relations also permeate and structure the division of labor in the workplace and in the distinction between "productive" paid labor, such that men tend to predominate in the higher-paid, manufacturing or professional occupations, and women in the lower-paid "pink collar" and service occupations, resulting in "a political–economic structure that generates gender-specific modes of exploitation, marginalization, and deprivation" (Fraser 1997, 19–20).

Gender inequalities also lead to the construction of androcentric norms that devalue women and are at the root of much of the harm they are subjected to, such as "sexual assault, sexual exploitation, and pervasive domestic violence; trivializing, objectifying, and demeaning stereotypical depictions in the media, harassment and disparagements in all spheres of everyday life, exclusion or marginalization in public spheres and deliberate bodies, and denial of full legal rights and equal protections" (Ibid.).

As Barbara Ehrenreich argued, a Marxist feminist standpoint must be predicated on the premise that in a capitalist society gender domination is inherently linked to class and class struggle. This is the case even if not all women's struggles are inherently anticapitalist and only seek to advance the interests of some special groups of women, and all class struggles are necessarily antisexist so long as they cling to patriarchal values. But, to the extent that class struggles aim to achieve the social and cultural autonomy of the working class, they are inherently linked to the struggle for women's liberation (Ehrenreich 1997, 69–70).

Susan Moller Okin is certainly right to point out that insofar as the "social structures that depend on a gendered division of labor are still in place, so long as women continue to bear disproportionate responsibility for domestic work, raising children, and caring for the sick and elderly, and so long as this work is privatized, undervalued, and unpaid or underpaid, the anticase principle will continue to be violated and women will remain systematically disadvantaged" (Okin 1994, 42). The social structures in question that need to be transformed are the capitalist relations of exploitation of men and women predicated on the private ownership of the means of production.

The implications of the foregoing discussion are clear. To succeed in "putting gender out of business," as Fraser put it, a radical feminist movement and project must reject what she calls the neoliberal, individualist, meritocratic cosmopolitan "ethos centered on diversity, women's empowerment, and LGBT rights" for equal treatment that came to replace "the more expansive, anti-hierarchical, egalitarian, class-sensitive, anti-capitalist understandings that had flourished in the 1960s and 1970s." This displacement is understandable, if misguided, because to a certain extent the politics of recognition "represent genuinely emancipatory responses to serious injustices that cannot be remedied by redistribution alone. Culture is a legitimate, even necessary, terrain of struggle, a sight of injustice in its own right and deeply imbricated with economic injustice" (Fraser 2000, 109). She insists that the objective of the struggle for a radical alternative is not only to dissolve 'identity politics' into 'class politics' but to "identify the shared roots of class and status injustices in capitalism, and to build alliances among those who must join together to fight against both of them" (Fraser 2017).

III: CLASS AND GENDER IN HAITI

The most recent 1987 Constitution of Haiti grants all Haitian adults (18 years or older) full equality before the law regardless of gender. It also declares that the family, whether it is constituted through marriage or the common practice of plaçage, is the fundamental unit of society, and that the state must provide for maternity, infants, and old age, and establish the paternity of children (Moïse 1990, 498).

There is a vast gulf between these desiderata and the social conditions most Haitian men, women, and children live under. As I have shown in the preceding chapters, Haiti is a highly unequal society wherein the top 1 percent that appropriates much of the wealth and has 50 times more resources/assets than the bottom 10 percent comprise the men and women of the ruling class. They own the principal means of production such as the major industries and businesses as well as the larger estates (40 hectares/99 acres or larger). The 10 percent who appropriate nearly 50 percent of the national income could be considered a middle class comprised of professional men and women, both in the urban and rural sectors; owners of smaller businesses; managers of public utilities, companies, and services; and public and government officials. As Beverly Bell noted, Haiti has a good record relative to world standards of appointing women to high office (Bell 2001, 149–150). In 2014, 8 of 23 ministers and 3 of 20 secretaries of state were women, as were 12 percent of all mayors. But they represent only 2.7 percent of the members of parliament, notwithstanding the 30 percent quota for women in all public offices stipulated by an amendment to the Constitution that has never been implemented (World Bank 2014, 39). Thus, their higher percentage in appointed political offices notwithstanding, their dismal representation in parliament (when that institution functions) means that they are in a weaker position to push for and enact legislation to address their demands for greater social and economic equality and opportunity.

It is also well known that those who occupy high office augment their salaries by appropriating funds from the public treasury illegally. These practices are also reinforced by the system of patronage, which, as Alexis Gardella put it, functions at all levels of Haitian society. While they can be beneficial to those in the lower classes, they remain, "a system of exclusion to the detriment of those not already in positions of economic and political power, and a serious constraint to social, legal and economic equity" (Gardella 2006, 15).

Another important characteristic of the bourgeoisie and the middle class is its division into mulatto—including Creole whites and Levantine immigrants who intermarried with Haitians and represent 5 percent of the population (Central Intelligence Agency 2020)—and black factions, and their corresponding ideologies of color that redefined the racist ideologies of the colonial era to justify and legitimize their respective claims to political power and dominance. As I have also shown previously, the dividing line between who was mulatto or black was not always easily drawn, but these classifications tended to coincide with one's class position in such a way that those of lighter skin complexion tended to be members of the dominant classes and wealthier than those of the poorer sectors of the population. Moreover, to ensure the generational reproduction of these categories, elite mulattoes tended to exclude individuals with nonidentifiable mulatto or white lineages from their social circles and as "proper" partners for marriage. Black elites also tended to avoid marrying those considered "unknowns," or who did "not belong" to that elite. Philippe-Richard Marius clarified that point succinctly when he argued that

> Class is a prior modality that contains color. In the class, the forms of color and concomitant forms of colorism are historically specific to it. Bilingual light skin Haitians of means and bi-lingual dark skin Haitians of means become, respectively, mulattoes and blacks only in the privileged classes. Similarly complexioned people in the working classes and the lumpenproletariat are simply malere, poor people, whose skin tones are socially invisible to the privileged. (2022, 201)

The key point here is that neither faction ever became hegemonic socially, ideologically, economically, or politically, and hence could not crystallize their respective ideologies of color into structures of exclusion and discrimination (Dupuy 2014, 79–80).

The men and women of the Haitian ruling class and members of the upper ranks of the middle class comprise both urban and rural components. In the rural areas, about 2 percent of them are large landlords who employ wage laborers or sharecroppers to work their land and sell their crops to local merchants and the export houses in urban centers. Among that dominant group are also to be found members of the local political elite and public administrators. Local merchants, with their patrons in the regional/local public administrations also use extra-market mechanisms to control the prices of the crops sold to them by their peasant clients. In the urban centers of Port-au-Prince and other major cities like Cap Haïtien, mulattoes and Creole whites own and control the major industrial, commercial, and import/export firms, including the assembly industries that became the most important industrial sector since the 1970s (Charles 1995, 142–143).

Conditions are very different for the bottom 90 percent of the population that comprise the urban and rural working classes, and the peasantry. According to the World Bank, 52 percent of the total population of 10.4 million lived in rural areas in 2012 (World Bank 2014, 11, 38). Of that population, 58.5 percent were poor, 23.8 percent, extremely poor; 2.5 million, below the extreme poverty line; and 6.3 million could not meet their basic needs. In terms of the geographic distribution of the poor and extremely poor, more than 80 percent live in rural areas, with the North and Northwest accounting for over 40 percent of the total (or 20 percent of the overall extreme poor), and 38 percent of that population were unable to meet their nutritional needs. By contrast, 12 percent of the extremely poor live in urban areas and 5 percent, in the Port-au-Prince metropolitan area.

As I show more fully in the next chapter, the political and economic crisis caused by the assassination of President Jovenel Moïse in 2021 and the rise of criminal gangs that are kidnapping, killing, and displacing thousands of citizens from their homes have exacerbated conditions for the most vulnerable sectors of the population such that in 2023, 31 percent of the population of 11.5 million were living on less than $2.15/day, and nearly 5 million were food insecure (UN Humanitarian 2023).

The poor in Haiti have become reliant on the remittances Haitian emigrants send to their families. Between 2001 and 2012 the share of households receiving private transfers domestically and mainly from the United States and the Dominican Republic increased from 42 to 69 percent (Ibid.). In 2020, such transfers accounted for 25 percent of Haiti's gross domestic product and nearly twice as much as the combined value of its exports and foreign direct investment (Central Intelligence Agency 2020).

Poor women and girls face greater difficulties in accumulating human capital despite significant progress in education and overall health outcomes. There is a strong positive correlation between education at all levels and the reduction of poverty (World Bank 2005, 26). Adult women continue to be less well educated than men and have higher levels of illiteracy and less access to health services, and they face higher obstacles in participating in the labor market. Most of the poor work, but they don't earn enough to escape poverty. This is especially so if they work in the primary agricultural sector where they earn on average 20 percent less than in the formal (public or private) sector. There are greater employment opportunities in urban areas, but jobs are still scarce and relatively low paid. Overall, 40 percent of the population is unemployed, as are 50 percent of the female workforce and 60 percent of youths. Sixty percent of working-age individuals (15–64) participate in the labor market, and 60 percent of those working earn below the minimum wage (World Bank 2014, 24–25).

Such a large unemployed population amounts to a vast reserve army of labor, which makes it possible for employers to have a great advantage in exploiting their workers by paying them poverty wages and denying them the most elementary labor rights. Faced with limited alternatives to provide for their needs, these workers are compelled to sell their labor power well below their value if they are able to find employment. As Marx put it, the larger the reserve army of labor is in proportion to the active labor force, the more those who are working are exploited: "This is the absolute general law of capital accumulation" (Marx 1976, 1, 798).

The household remains the primary locus where men exercise power, authority, and violence over women and their children, especially girls. It is the site where the "struggles for survival shape gender disparity" and where the "inequality and violence perpetuated ultimately impair girls' and women's status within the Haitian hierarchies and generate patterns of gender-based violence in the public sphere" (Duramy 2014, 39–40; Charles 1995, 142). Gender-based violence is indeed pervasive in Haiti. In 2012, 13 percent of women reported having experienced sexual violence, and 29 percent of married women have experienced emotional, physical, or sexual spousal violence (Duramy 2014, 39–40). In 2023, the gangs that have been kidnapping, killing, and displacing thousands from their homes, especially in the poorest areas of Port-au-Prince, have openly raped women and young girls to instill fear among the communities under their control. As Megan Janetsky and Fernanda Pesce put it, "sexual violence has long been used as an instrument of war around the world, a barbaric way to sow terror in communities and assert control" (Janetsky and Pesce 2023).

Men- and women-headed households account for 59 percent of the poor, and 43 percent of that population live in women-headed households. On average, nonpoor households comprise four persons, poor households have 5.3 persons, and 80 percent of those households have five or more (World Bank 2014, 24–25). Yet in contrast to women-headed households, those headed by men in rural areas were four times more likely to face food insecurity than female-headed households. Gardella attributed this difference to the fact that because women have traditionally been engaged in food production, they were more likely than male-headed households to focus on ensuring food security for their family, and they also have more access than men to petty commercial activities to generate income. In general, poor rural households tend to be better off than those in urban areas. This is not because peasant farmers in Haiti produce primarily for their subsistence but instead sell their crops in both rural and urban markets for the highest prices they can obtain. Women then buy the lowest-priced food items for domestic consumption (Gardella 2006, 12).

At the same time, when conditions become desperate and reach critical survival thresholds in poor households, especially if the men abandon their families and are unable or unwilling to provide for their children, and the women are unable to do so on their own, it is usually they who decide to send, in effect sell, their children for a pittance to work as unpaid living servants in wealthier households in urban areas through the practice known as restavèk (stay/live with). Under such conditions the children, both girls and boys, are subject to abuse and violence. A recent study of this practice estimated that between 150,000 and 500,000 children in Haiti were living in servitude, and 17.4 percent of females and 12.2 percent of males reported having been restavèks before age 18. In addition to never having attended school, female restavèks were more likely to report that they had experienced physical, emotional, and sexual violence (Gilbert et al. 2018, 184–185; de Hoog 2017, 9).

Notwithstanding current laws against such practices that require hosting families to pay these children for their services, they are either abandoned by their hosts on the street or kept working for free, a relationship that may justifiably be likened to a modern form of indentured servitude or slavery (Bell 2016). A similar situation exists in the Dominican Republic, where poor Haitian mothers also engage in trafficking their children across the border illegally are then forced to work and are often abused in Dominican households or in those of Haitian migrant workers in the bateyes (the sugar company compounds). As is the case in Haiti, Dominican law prohibits such practices for immigrant Haitian and Dominican children, but they are not enforced (Shoaff 2017, 450–451).

About 80 percent of those who live in rural areas have access to land and 82 percent among them own their plots, with the rest being rented through the metayage system. These relatively small lands of 1.8 hectares (4.5 acres) on average that peasants own tend to be fragmented and dispersed, but those who own more than two hectares (5 acres) tend to have lower incidence of poverty. Some 40 percent of these landowners do not have titles or sales receipts for their properties (World Bank 2005, 22). Men and women inherit property, as do children from their parents. But women tend to receive smaller shares of properties and face higher obstacles than their male counterparts in the process (Gardella 2006, 15).

The significance of the distinction between those who own and possess land (without titles for their property) and those who rent land through the métayage or sharecropping system is that the former two categories are not only more secure financially but also more independent because they own their own tools/equipment and draft animals. In other words, they are not exploited by the landed bourgeoisie or better-off farmers who own or lease their land, and they produce and sell their food crops in a rural or urban market and for export. But insofar as they rely on local and urban intermediaries to sell their crops, they are subject to price manipulations by the latter.

By contrast, those who have access to land only through the métayage or the sharecropping system are exploited by the landowners who extract rents from their tenants. Tenant farmers usually pay a fixed rent to the landowner in advance for a year or more, but sharecroppers pay their rent in money or in kind at the time of the harvest and which tend to be higher than those paid by tenant farmers. Below the categories with access to land are the landless, who are hired as day laborers by the larger landowners and must be included among the rural proletariat (Dupuy 2014, 121–122).

There is a clear division of labor in agricultural production and commercialization. Most farmers diversify their crops such as bananas, mangoes, maize, cassava, yams, peanuts, and coffee, for an average of five per farm, with 70 percent producing at least four crops, depending on the size of the farm (World Bank 2014, 55). Men engage in the heavier agricultural labor (e.g., clearing and tilling the land; harvesting; taking care of livestock, cattle, and horses; cultivating and marketing export crops; and doing agricultural wage-labor work). Women, on the other hand, are involved in seeding, planting, weeding, and harvesting; caring for small livestock (pigs, goats, poultry); selling crops in a market; buying essential goods for the household; and cooking, cleaning, and caring for children, the elderly, and the sick. In short, women perform both unpaid domestic as well as income-generating labor. While they "are marginalized in relation to their male counterparts at the same time [they] exercise a considerable degree of autonomy and independence in the management of the household's resources" (World Bank 2014, 55). This is because the domestic market, both rural and urban, "is almost entirely run through female konmèsan from the smallest corner to the local and regional markets, finally to the big market in Port-au-Prince, and back down again" (Charlmers et al. 2020, 19).

These processes may be illustrated by looking at the production and commercialization of peanuts and mangoes. Peanut production is mostly undertaken by relatively small-scale farmers, and women normally process, transport, and sell the peanuts in markets throughout the country. Overall, about 35,000 farmers are involved in its production on plots ranging from 0.1 and 0.5 hectare (0.25 to 1.2 acres) using mostly family labor to clear the land and dry and store the nuts. They sell some 95 percent of their crops and use the remaining 5 percent for new seeds and personal consumption. Although peanut processing occurs in all areas where it is grown, most of it is concentrated in urban/suburban areas. The processing of peanuts into peanut butter (manba) is carried out by thousands of small and large enterprises in all regions of the country using both manual and mechanized processors (Ibid.).

The division of labor between men and women in this sector is like that for other crops. Men do 70 percent of the labor of preparing the soil, planting the seeds, cultivating, and harvesting the peanuts, and women do the other 30 percent. But women do the marketing, either alone or through women intermediaries known as madansara, who transport the unshelled peanuts to be processed and sold. In short, "economically speaking, peanuts represent a significant source of income for farmers, processors, and above all women, who account for 80% of the people selling peanuts on a retail basis (grilled nuts, manba, peanut brittle, etc.)." Even if peanut earnings alone are not sufficient to cover their living expenses and they must pursue other income-earning activities, most of the women (74 percent) said they were satisfied with their activity and able to achieve a measure of economic empowerment and financial independence that allowed them to cover some household expenses and (re)invest their profits (Jayaram 2018, 473–475). In other words, farming women can exercise considerable control over the income they generate through their labor rather than surrendering them to men.

Similarly, there is a clear gendered division of labor in the production of mangoes for both export and as a cash crop for domestic consumption. The harvesting of mangoes involves two distinct processes. One is to pick the mangoes from the trees and drop them into the hands of a catcher. The latter normally uses a sack stretched outward and places the mangoes with the stems pointing downward toward the ground when it is full to prevent damaging them. After the stems are removed, the mangoes are then washed, dried, and stored to get them ready to be sold.

Men do the harvesting on their own land using family labor or hiring pickers if they earn enough to pay them. Women wash and dry the mangoes and sometimes catch them. Young boys can also catch and pick the mangoes if they're old enough, and they wash and dry them along with young girls. Women rarely do the picking unless they can do so with a picking pole (keyèt) designed for that purpose if the mangoes are close enough to the ground. As with other domestic crops, women bring the mangoes to market to sell them (Ibid.).

In urban areas, by contrast, women generally face different conditions because the unemployment rate is almost double that of the rural areas (39.6 percent and 22.3 percent, respectively), and employment rates are also lower. Metropolitan areas with the largest populations (Port-au-Prince, Cap Haïtien) have lower employment rates and the highest unemployment rates in contrast to those urban areas with less population (World Bank 2014, 38). All other factors being equal in the urban areas, women are 6 percent more likely to earn less than the minimum wage than men, regardless of the type of industry in which they're employed.

Moreover gender, age, and education are important determinants of employment in the formal or informal sectors, such that all other things being equal, women are 6 percent more likely to find employment in the informal than in the formal sector. Education especially is the highest predictor of employment in these two sectors: Whereas those with higher education (upper secondary or higher) are 40 times more likely to be employed in the formal than in the informal sector, those with lower-secondary education are 20 times more likely to be similarly employed. Those with a primary education are likely to earn 30 percent more per hour, 50 percent more for those with a secondary education, and 125 percent more for those with upper secondary education or higher. Those with five additional years of experience earn 15 percent more per hour.

These factors, however, do not apply to women equally. Women are 20 percent more likely to be unemployed than men and 6 percent more likely to be in the informal than in the formal sector, and they earn 32 percent less than men, ceteris paribus, even accounting for the number of children in the household. As the World Bank put it, "over two-thirds of this difference is unexplained by observable characteristics, suggesting that discrimination could play a role in accounting for the results" (Ibid., 66). Those unobservable characteristics are none other than the institutionalized structures of discrimination that ideologies that devalue women attempt to legitimize.

Women are also overwhelmingly concentrated in the trade sector where they account for over 70 percent of those jobs but earn less than half of those employed in education, health care, transportation, and construction that have more managerial and executive positions and require more qualified and semiqualified workers. In short, "trade and self-employment are, respectively, the industry and the occupation with the largest numbers and percentages of women, the poor, the least well-paid, and the least well-educated workers in urban Haiti" (World Bank 2014, 70). Women and men who are not self-employed or engaged in other income-generating employment in the formal and informal sectors in urban or rural areas resort to what Anglade has labeled the "ghetto" of domestic services in middle- and upper-class households, even though she only considers women as comprising such workers (Anglade 1986, 215).

As was the case in other underdeveloped countries where wages are low, the World Bank and the United States Agency for International Development pressed the government of Jean-Claude Duvalier to embrace that industry as a development strategy in the 1970s, but it was not until the 1980s that the country did so fully. Foreign investors were attracted to Haiti for a number of reasons: its abundant supply of unskilled, low-wage workers kept in check with violent repression; its close proximity to the US market; its lack of foreign exchange controls and other kinds of government interference; its policies allowing the free circulation of the US dollar; its tax incentives with exemptions on income and profits; and its tariff exemptions on imported raw materials, machinery, or other inputs used in the assembly industries as well as on the export of the assembled products (Ch. 2, and Dupuy 2005, 64–65).

Although Port-au-Prince was and remains the epicenter of that industry in Haiti, it subsequently expanded to other parts of the country. In the early 2000s, the World Bank and the Inter-American Development Bank helped finance the creation of free-trade zones in the northeast region of Haiti near the border with the Dominican Republic. Doing so required the eviction of hundreds of peasant farmers in the fertile agricultural region of the Maribahoux plains and the appropriation of more than a thousand acres of their farms to build the 246-acre Caracol Industrial Park for the Korean-owned clothing manufacturer Sea-A Trading Co., Ltd., and 251 acres to build a power plant and a deepwater port to support the park (Ibid.; Steckley and Shamsie 2015, 189).

The United States and the international financial institutions (World Bank, Inter-American Development Bank, United States Agency for International Development) continued to recommend the same failed policies after the devastating earthquake that shook Haiti in 2010. In response to it, the United States devised a Haiti Economic Lift Program (HELP) that extended the trade benefits of the 2006 Haiti Hemispheric Opportunity through Partnership Encouragement Act (HOPE) designed to boost clothing exports by increasing tariff preferences and expanding duty-free exemptions for textile and apparel products (Steckley and Shamsie 2015, 188).

As expected, the claims about the development potentials of the assembly industry to generate sustainable development in Haiti never materialized. They were not meant to. Notwithstanding the World Bank's acknowledgment that this strategy was not living up to expectations, it continued to advocate it as a solution (Dupuy 2014, 102–103). The primary reason for investing in Haiti was to take advantage of its low-paid labor and to extract the maximum profits possible for both foreign and domestic investors. The low wages the workers in that industry earned were insufficient to increase demand for domestic consumer goods that could be produced locally and stimulate investments in more capital-intensive industries, whether they were foreign- or Haitian-owned. Consequently, the profits appropriated by the foreign-owned and -managed firms were repatriated and not reinvested in Haiti, and Haitian entrepreneurs also sought opportunities elsewhere where the returns on their investments were greater (Dupuy 2014, 121–122).

The assembly industry did not contribute to solving the chronic unemployment problem in Haiti. As of April 2019, that industry employed 60,000 workers, with women comprising 68 percent of its labor force (Ibid.; Djaya et al., 2019, 15; Germain 2019). In November of that year, and notwithstanding the opposition of the Association des Industries d'Haïti (ADIH—Association of Haitian Industries) that such an increase would jeopardize jobs, the government of Jovenel Moïse signed into law the new minimum wage of 500–550 gourdes ($4.64–$5.10) for an eight-hour day. That increase amounted to less than half what the unions representing the workers demanded and which, due to inflation and the devaluation of the gourde vis-à-vis the US dollar, is insufficient to cover their basic needs. It needs pointing out, moreover, that this wage is equivalent to what it was in 2010 accounting for the rate of inflation and the relation of the gourde to the US dollar at the time (Dupuy 2014, 121–122; Jeanty 2019; Charlmers 2019).

Even if it could be shown that there is no baseline statistically significant difference by gender for average pay in the assembly industry in Haiti, women with children report lower take-home pay than women without children largely because of incorrect payments of maternity benefits, changes in seniority during maternity leave, or not receiving payments during breastfeeding breaks while at work (Djaya et al. 2019, 13). Women are also subjected to sexual harassment and abuse, such as being coerced by male supervisors to sleep with them to keep their jobs. Equally as significant when workers receive wage increases in the factories, employers raise the daily per-unit production quotas (e.g., the number of bras or pajamas), thereby forcing the workers to put in more hours to meet them without receiving overtime pay (Bell and Erket 2013). As Marx observed poignantly, "the abuse of the labour of women by the sheer brutality of overwork" is fundamental to capitalist exploitation (Marx 1976, 1, 599).

As the Other Worlds report asked pertinently, "Why would anyone take such a job?" to which the women who were posed that question responded: "because they needed jobs." The report further noted that "in a country with about 40% unemployment, any amount of money on payday might stave off starvation, even though the worker loses over the long term" (Bell and Erket 2013). The Haitian (and foreign) owners of those industries know that all too well. As the manager of a plant put it: "If you don't work, you don't have anything. With the wages they get at least they can survive. It's better than nothing" (Ayti Kale Je/Haiti Grassroots Watch 2011). The owners of these industries understand well how the absolute law of capital accumulation works.

IV: WHAT IS TO BE DONE?

Poor women from the working and peasant classes are the most oppressed, discriminated against, and exploited sectors of Haitian society. But it does not follow that women in general work for the benefit and enrichment of men in general. As Gracita Osias, a woman interviewed by Beverly Bell, said: "In Haiti, not all women are exploited. Some are exploiters," and to which Evelyne Attis, another interviewee, said about bourgeois women: "look how they treat their maids. Those rich ladies have much more in common with their menfolk than with us poor women" (Bell and Erket 2013).

An important distinction needs to be made between the situation working class women face in the rural versus the urban areas. In the former, where most of the peasant farmers own (or control) their own land, men and women engage in the production of food for the domestic and export markets in the context of the division of labor outlined above. In contrast to those farmers who rent their land from landlords and pay rents, the majority who own/control/work their land (whether they have titles), and sometimes hire day laborers, are to be considered more as commodity producers for the market who directly appropriate the fruits of their labor than as directly exploited by capitalists.

The gains from their labor (food crops principally) are low, and they remain poor primarily because they continue to work on small plots of land with primitive technology and don't control the sale prices for their goods.

And when they rely on intermediaries (the madansaras) to carry and sell their crops, they earn still less than they would otherwise. That is because, as Matts Lundahl explained, there is a high degree of competition between the farmers and the madansaras, and as a result, the profit margins for the former are very low. Hence, the competition among peasants and the madansaras is intense, and prices are not only a reflection of it but also express the credit available to the peasants and the terms on which they can get them (Lundahl 1983, 27).

Nonetheless, women who sell the crops that both they and their male partners produce can exercise a certain degree of control and autonomy over their income rather than turning it over to the men in their lives. This is clearly expressed in the fact that rural households headed by men are four times more likely to face food insecurity than those headed by women, and of the 59 percent of the population who live in male- and female-headed households, 57 percent of them live in male-headed households.

By contrast, the situation of working-class women is worse in urban areas, where they are 20 percent more likely to be unemployed than men; are more likely to work in the informal trade sector than in the formal commercial, industrial, and public sectors where they earn significantly less than men; and form the majority of those employed as domestics in wealthier households, where wages are low. Thus, it can be said, men in general benefit from the discrimination against women in general insofar as the former have more access to education and get paid higher wages for doing the same work, ceteris paribus, and from the free, "unproductive" childcare and household labor women perform in male-headed households. But the men and women who profit from and are enriched by the labor of men and women are the capitalists who employ them in their businesses, large or small, in urban or rural areas.

What, then, is to be done? A Marxist analysis of gender divisions and inequalities in a capitalist society must be linked to the class relations and exploitation that are inherent to that social system. Transforming the latter was a necessary starting point to achieving the former. More important, however, is that women activists involved in the feminist struggles for gender equality in Haiti came to the same conclusion.

As Carolle Charles has shown, during the 1980s, and especially after the fall of the Duvalier regime in 1986, many women's organizations and feminist groups, inspired and in many cases influenced by the broader international women's movement, including Haitian women immigrants who returned to

Haiti to participate in this struggle, introduced women's demands into the political agenda. The women's groups and organizations reflected the class differences and divisions in Haiti and had different goals and objectives. Some emphasized demands for basic services, such as health care, reducing infant mortality, and providing education to the poor, while others focused on issues of survival, jobs, and socioeconomic change and the recognition of women as equal citizens. Charles argued that the women's movement was "part of a struggle to redefine civil society and a more egalitarian and democratic society in a country characterized by exclusion, poverty, and extreme repression of the majority of its population. The women's struggles are part of what has made Haitian women into a new collective subject of social change" (Charles 1995, 155, 158).

As both Charles and Bell pointed out, the demands for radical change and a thorough restructuring of Haiti into a more democratic, more just, and more equal society began to be formulated in late 1986 after the fall of the Duvalier regime and were part of the movement that brought Jean-Bertrand Aristide to power in February 1991. That movement and its activists were severely crushed after the coup d'état that toppled Aristide seven months after he took office by the military dictatorship that ruled until October 1994 (Dupuy 2007). Yet even within that brief period, Aristide's government implemented some significant reforms that benefited women directly, such as a basic needs program for poor women and children, increasing government spending in health care, immunization, education, potable water, electricity, judicial reform, and rural infrastructure. His administration also created the Ministry on the Status and Rights of Women to address and respond to violence against women; to facilitate women's access to credit, education, and better working conditions; to support initiatives by women's organizations to advance women's rights and equality; and to promote programs in education, culture, the economy, the law, and protection against domestic violence (Bell 2001, 155–156).

It is evident that based on more recent data on the condition of women in Haiti, these important initiatives were not sustained. Significantly, the conclusions reached by Solidarity Among Haitian Women (SOFA) and other women's organizations because of these struggles were that "the problem of women is the problem of the masses" and that "class exploitation and repressive and unresponsive government, combined with patriarchy, form the bases of their oppression" (Bell 2001, 151). As Bell went on to point out, poor women came to see that they were not "a class in themselves but rather as an especially oppressed group within the labor and peasant classes; that class and gender are interrelated sites of struggle [and that] their absolute and relative status will improve only as a result of changes in both areas" (Bell 2001, 152).

To that end, Bell summarized the demands of the women's groups for social change that address the need to achieve two major transformations in Haitian society. On the one hand, they include demands for child support, greater control over household incomes, greater access to credit and protection for their property, an end to psychological and physical domestic abuse and rape, and the right of women to assemble and speak freely. In essence they speak to the need to transform the patriarchal structures of the household as the primary cite where men have traditionally exercised power, violence, and dominance over women, and allow women to have and exercise a greater degree of autonomy. On the other hand, they also include demands to refute the logic of capitalism and commercialism, to end poverty and meet basic needs, for the state to assume ownership of the principal industries and utilities, to prioritize domestic-led development and self-sufficient agriculture, to reject the premise that Haiti is a source of cheap labor for foreign investors, and to provide for the basic needs of all citizens, all of which are essential to transforming the extant relations of exploitation by both foreign and domestic capital. (Bell 2001, 195–197).

Taken together, then, these demands point to a maximalist democracy (or democratic socialism), that is, a democracy that empowers the people rather than the propertied classes and foreign investors, and hence leads to a more just and egalitarian society (Dupuy 2007). No one can enjoy any right, such as civil and political rights, unless that individual also has the essentials for a healthy and active life. As such, the demands of the women's movement are at one with those spelled out in the Montana Accord that called for a thorough transformation of the state to prioritize and serve the interests of the majority rather than those of the bourgeoisie and their foreign overlords (Commission 2021).

NOTES

1. I distinguish between "wealth" and "income." The former is derived from one's assets, investments, and/or exploitation of the labor of others; the latter is what one earns from one's services to or labor for others.

2. The distinction here is between a wage laborer who is hired by an employer and receives a salary in return and who is also free to leave that employment for whatever reason, and a slave, who is bought by and belongs to the slave owner, for whom they are compelled to work without compensation.

3. To be sure, these norms have been and continue to be challenged and have led to changes within middle- and working-class households, wherein men now also share household and parental responsibilities, hence the concern mentioned above by the Catholic Church and other institutions that resist them to maintain the traditional gender roles and prevent "gender confusion."

4

Whither Haiti after Moïse?

I

On July 7, 2021, Haitian president Jovenel Moïse was assassinated in his residence in Pétion-Ville, a relatively affluent city of 374,000 people east of the capital city of Port-au-Prince, by a group of assailants who met little resistance from his security guards. Elected in 2016 to succeed President Michel Martelly, Moïse did not take office until a year later due to delays in reviewing and certifying his victory. He was the third president to have been assassinated since Haiti won its independence in 1804. But in contrast to Jean-Jacques Dessalines, Haiti's first head of state, who was assassinated in 1806, and Vilbrun Guillaume Sam, Haiti's 24th president, in 1915, Moïse was the first to be killed by a group comprised of Haitian, Columbian, and Haitian American mercenaries. Their objective was reportedly to obtain the list of those in Haiti and abroad who were involved in drug trafficking and which Moïse was allegedly going to turn over to US authorities. He had also nationalized a seaport that was used to smuggle drugs into the country and destroyed an airstrip that served the same purpose. Moïse, in short, "threatened many of the economic elite, including a number of people with deep criminal connections" (Abi-Habib 2021).

To put the assassination of Moïse in the broader context of Haiti's tumultuous political history, it had 24 heads of state between 1804 and 1915. One committed suicide, 2 were assassinated, 14 were overthrown, 5 died in office, and 2 completed their terms (Dupuy 1989, 118). The United States invaded Haiti in 1915 and occupied it until 1934, during which time there were four presidents. The last president elected under the occupation in 1930 governed until 1941. And from 1941 to 2021 there were 21 presidents.[1] Four of them were overthrown, and one other, Jean-Bertrand Aristide, was overthrown twice.

For over a year, Jovenel Moïse, who assumed the presidency in February 2017, had been plagued by an opposition seeking to remove him from office. From mid-September to early December 2019, the country was gripped by massive and at times violent and deadly demonstrations in the capital city of Port-au-Prince and other provincial cities demanding his resignation. The demonstrators referred to the country as being "lok"—a Haitian Creole term for "locked down"—as demonstrators blocked roads and burned tires, uncollected debris, and garbage that forced schools and businesses to close (Regan 2019, 2–8).

The immediate cause of the demonstrations was the severe shortage of gasoline and diesel fuel that led to long lines of cars, trucks, buses, and taxis at gas stations because of the government's decision to stop selling them at a subsidized price to distributors, thereby making life even more difficult for most of the population already facing hardships. The outrage against the government was also fueled by reports and human rights groups that some $2 billion had been diverted from the agreement the Venezuelan government of President Hugo Chavez had entered with Haitian president René Préval in 2006. Known as the Petrocaribe fund, that agreement allowed Haiti to repay Venezuela the fuel it sold to Haiti within three months based on the price of a barrel of gas on the world market at the time. Haiti could also keep a percentage of the amount due to Venezuela as a long-term loan to be repaid at very low interest rates or do so in kind, such as agricultural products or other goods made in Haiti (Regan 2019; *Le Monde* 2019).

With Venezuela facing its own economic and political crisis since Nicolas Maduro was reelected in 2018, the Petrocaribe agreement with Haiti also ended that year. President Moïse then turned to the International Monetary Fund (IMF) for financial assistance. In typical IMF modus operandi, it demanded that the Haitian government end its fuel subsidies, thereby causing an increase in fuel prices at the pump (PBS News Hour 2019). Raising those prices may have played a role in sparking the protests, but the underlying causes were rooted in the glaring social and economic inequalities, the crushing poverty of the majority, and the corruption and impunity of elected officials of the previous Martelly government and that of President Moïse, both from the same Pati Ayisyen Tèt Kalé.[2] The main causes of the opposition to Moïse, however, were his use of gangs to crush his opponents in their strongholds in the poorest sections of Port-au-Prince, such as in La Saline in 2018, Bel Air in 2019, and Cité Soleil in 2020. The assailants reportedly killed at least 240 people, raped many women, and burned hundreds of homes in the targeted areas (Coto 2019; Harvard Law School 2021, 3–5; Katz 2022).

To win the support of US president Donald Trump, Moïse voted with the United States at the meeting of the Organization of American States in January 2019 to not recognize the new Maduro government. In return for his fealty, Trump allegedly promised Moïse to help him stay in office until his five-year term ended in 2022 (*Haiti en Marche* 2019). For their part, opposition groups and individuals (including those from civil society, religious denominations, women's organizations, peasant groups, labor unions, and the private sector) announced an agreement in early November 2019 to choose a Supreme Court judge to serve as interim president until new elections could be held. But knowing that he had the backing of the United States, he and his ruling PHTK rejected that agreement (*Haiti en Marche* 2019).

Neither the demonstrators nor the opposition threatened Moïse's grip on power if he had the support of the United States, and they eventually dissipated (Coto 2019). Even if the underlying factors that sparked the protests ran deeply into the socioeconomic structures of Haitian society and the oppressive conditions under which most of the population lived, this was not a social movement for fundamental, radical social change as was the popular democratic movement that led to the ouster of Jean-Claude Duvalier in 1986 and the election of Jean-Bertrand Aristide, a former priest and advocate of Liberation Theology, in 1990. That movement never realized its objectives, but it was a warning to the dominant classes and their international overlords that the Haitian people could rise again someday to build a more just and democratic society that prioritized their interests rather than those of domestic and foreign capitalists (Dupuy 2019, esp. Ch. 3).

It was in this context that Prime Minister Ariel Henry became the new head of government pledging to bring Moïse's killers to justice and putting an end to the armed gangs who are spreading havoc in the capital city of

Port-au-Prince and other parts of the country. As Daniel Foote, a former US special envoy sent to Haiti by President Joseph Biden to help restore peace and organize new democratic elections noted, "a group of foreign powers led by the United States moved fast to appoint Henry, the former social affairs minister, as acting prime minister" (Foote 2023).

According to *The New York Times* and *CNN*, "Haitian investigators believe that Henry was involved both in the planning of the assassination and a subsequent cover-up," a charge he denied. Judge Garry Orélien, then the highest-ranking justice supervising the dossier on the assassination, reportedly told CNN that "Ariel (Henry) is connected and friends with the mastermind of the assassination. They planned it with him. Ariel is a prime suspect in Jovenel Moïses's assassination, and he knows it." Realizing that he had been recorded, however, Orélien backtracked and said that he did not "recall talking to anyone about the case in great detail" and that "lots of people are trying to influence the case and I will not play their game" (Rivers et al., 2022; Kurmanaev 2022). Daniel Foote (2023) also alleged that Henry was "directly linked by phone records to those suspected of being behind Moïse's assassination."

But so far none of these allegations have been adjudicated in a court of law. As the report from the Institute for Justice & Democracy in Haiti (2023) pointed out, even though Henry's "de facto government is directly responsible for the corruption, impunity, and incompetence that underlies almost every component of Haiti's crises," he remains in power with the full support of the international community. He fired the prosecutors who had been looking into his possible role in Moïse's assassination. A third magistrate stepped down, and a fourth refused to take the case because he feared for his safety. Henry offered to send other suspects to US authorities if they asked him to do so. The Haitian Minister of Justice, however, was opposed to turning those suspects over to the United States because "it was not Americans who were killed" (Charles 2022, February 12).

On the other hand, two foreign suspects involved in the assassination turned themselves in to US authorities and were charged with murder and conspiracy (Ibid.). And the US Justice Department charged four men, including three Haitian American citizens and a Colombian citizen in connection with the assassination. In all so far, 11 people, mostly from Haiti, Colombia, and South Florida, have been charged and will face trials in Miami. Rodolphe Jaar, one of those charged in the assassination, was convicted and sentenced to life imprisonment by a federal court judge in Florida, and several others who have been apprehended and extradited to the United States possibly face similar sentences (Luscombe 2023).

Neither has Henry done anything to take on and prosecute the gangs, estimated to be as many as 200 (Espérance 2023, July 4; Anderson 2023), who continued to act with impunity as they had done under Moïse. As of June 2023, they controlled most of Port-au-Prince and engaged in widespread incidents of kidnappings and lynching for the first quarter of that year.

In addition to kidnapping and killing those who refused or were unable to pay the ransoms they demanded, the gangs raped or threatened to rape women and young girls to instill fear in and paralyze the people in the communities they controlled and among the general population (Janetsky and Pesce 2023). According to the Office of the High Commissioner for Human Rights, there were 1,119 kidnappings in 2022, and the Single Health Information System recorded 16,470 cases of gender-based violence (GBV), along with 949 cases of sexual violence. But the stigma victims of sexual violence face, the fear of retaliation by the perpetrators, and the lack of access to GBV services make it impossible to quantify the extent of such violence (Reliefweb 2023). It is worth noting, however, that while women and girls have been victimized by the gangs, many have also been actively involved in their criminal activities, including kidnappings, accompanying their male partners in some areas to raise less suspicion, carrying weapons, and stealing anything of value in the sites that are then set on fire (*Dominican Today* 2023).

In some neighborhoods of Port-au-Prince ordinary citizens defended themselves by attacking, killing, and lynching suspected gang members (Sanon 2023). Known as the "Bwa Kale" ("Sharp Stick") movement, it spread to 8 of the country's 10 departments and killed hundreds of suspected gang members. According to the Centre d'analyse et de recherche en droits de l'homme (CARDH [Center for Analysis and Research on Human Rights]), Bwa Kale began its counteroffensive against the gangs in April 2023 and has reportedly killed at least 160 alleged gang members in different parts of the country, most of them in the West department (where Port-au-Prince is). This counteroffensive led to a reduction in kidnappings in April and May, but 43 murders were registered during that time (CARDH 2023). In all, since January 2023, the gangs reportedly killed more than 2,400 people and kidnapped more than 950 people, amounting to an increase of 125 percent compared to the same time span in 2022. Another 5,000 have been forced to flee their neighborhoods, raising the total of internally displaced people to 200,000 (Al Jazeera 2023, May 3; Al Jazeera 2023, August 19; Charles 2023, February 8; Charles 2023, March 28; Charles 2023, August 28; Human Rights Watch 2023; Ioanes 2023; Johnston and François 2023, August 18; Lee 2023; Roth and Humayun 2023; UNICEF 2023).

A human rights activist, linking the surge of mob justice to "years of elite political corruption and connivance with organized crime," added: "it's harrowing; it's brutal; it's inhuman. But when you consider all these years that we have been under that pressure by the gangs, the economic people [and] the political people . . . it is not surprising!" (Isaac 2023). Or as others who have risen to combat the gangs put it, "our calls to the authorities fell on deaf ears. They don't listen to us. If the population doesn't stand up, more civilians will be killed" (Mérancourt and Coletta 2023).

The rise of the Bwa Kale movement led the Haitian human rights organization to raise the concern that this movement could also lead to targeting people who are mistakenly identified as gang members, thereby worsening the security crisis (Ibid.). A spokesman for the CARDH called on Haitian authorities and civilian groups "to work together to fight the gangs and avoid a cycle of increasingly brutal retaliation" and falling into an abyss of violence and destruction (Morland and Isaac 2023). Another member pointed out that while "the reaction of the population, after years of gangs imposing their law, can be attributed to self-defense, [the] gangs are supported by certain authorities, politicians, businesspeople. At almost all levels of the police force, gangs have links with police officers. The police do not have the means to confront the growing gangs systematically and simultaneously" (Morland and Isaac 2023). Yet from January to July 2023, the police arrested over 2,000 suspected gang members throughout the country and confiscated firearms and ammunitions, as well as kilos of drugs and cocaine and vehicles and boats, and recuperated stolen vehicles and thousands in Haitian gourdes and US currency from the gangs (Charles 2023, May 31; Blaise 2023).

Similarly, the Institute for Justice & Democracy in Haiti (2023) warned that understandable as it may be that the insecurity and humanitarian crises have driven local communities to defend themselves against suspected gang members and reduce kidnappings and other gang-related criminal activities, "the consequences for the rule of law and community reconciliation are potentially devastating." These uncontrolled developments and their deadly consequences, in short, are symptomatic of a state and government used for the pursuit of self-interest by those who control it rather than for the protection and welfare of its citizens. And as Roberson Alphonse (2023, July 20) pointed out, it is impossible to know how long this period of relative calm will last given that by late July 2023 the balance of forces between the police and the gangs had not been reversed decisively.

The United States and Canada imposed sanctions against many members of the government and the bourgeoisie they believed were supporting the gangs, including former president Michel Martelly, other prime ministers, and gang leader Chérizier for leading the two-month blockade of Haiti's main fuel terminal (Robertson 2023, January 12; *The Associated Press* 2023). The US Treasury Department designated four other individuals, including former senators, for their alleged involvement in drug trafficking and corruption. The United States also named and froze the assets of five Haitian nationals, four of whom were politicians, and barred them from traveling to the United States, and Canada did so for 17 Haitians, including 2 former presidents, 2 prime ministers, and 3 well-known businessmen for their alleged connections to the gangs, drug trafficking, and corruption. Canada imposed 26 economic sanctions while the United States issued travel bans on or froze the assets of five individuals. France also got a "common European policy" adopted that will make it possible for European countries to impose sanctions against Haitian individuals, and investigators from the United Nations are compiling a list of those who could be sanctioned and prevented from seeking refuge in any UN member country (Charles 2023, February 23; Charles 2023, June 23).

Canadian prime minister Trudeau remarked that "Canada has long recognized that much of the instability in Haiti comes from a small number of powerful lead families who are fomenting instability and financing violence for their own gains at terrible costs to the Haitian people" (Charles 2023, February 17). Marcus Garcia (2023, April 26) made the same point: "the root cause of the current crisis, well before the rapid and massive expansion of the murderous gangs, is to be found in this empty background, the looting of the public fund by those in power and their business allies." Monique Clesca (2023, March 10) put it starkly when she wrote: "Criminality is ubiquitous in Haitian officialdom. In fact, Haitian politics and government at all levels have become so enmeshed in and dependent on graft, gunrunning, drug smuggling, and gang violence that it is nearly impossible to disentangle them. All this depletes the state's capacity to provide critical social services for Haiti's more than 11 million people—that is, if the current leaders had any will to do so." Pierre Espérance (2023, July 4), the executive director of the National Human Rights Defense Network in Haiti, made the same point: "In Haiti, gang members are not independent warlords operating apart from the state. They are part of the way the state functions—and how political leaders assert power." In short, the sanctions may affect some of the targeted individuals who may lose access to the prebends of office and enrich themselves through what is known as "*la politique de doublure.*"[3] But they will not change the systemic structures and practices that (re)produce these outcomes, nor the balance of power between the bourgeoisie and the state, or between foreign or domestic capital and the workers they employ.[4]

Gangs also took control of other towns and communities in the north, west, and central parts of Haiti, where they continued to kidnap, rape, and kill citizens (Charles 2022, January 12; Charles 2023, January 5). They set up toll stations in roads throughout the country to force drivers, passengers, or motorcyclists to pay them to be allowed to proceed or risk getting killed *(New York Carib News* 2023, February 25). The Haitian police forces went on the offensive at the beginning of 2023, attacked gang strongholds in Port-au-Prince and several other cities and towns throughout the country, killed and arrested many of them, and intended to continue their offensive until the gangs were neutralized. But with only 9,700 active-duty police officers from a total of 15,000 five years ago, this is a daunting task, and some among them are alleged to be gang members. The gangs spread their violence more broadly and retaliated by killing 94 policemen since January 2023 (Sanon 2023, April 27; Woods 2023, March 18; Coto 2023, January 23; *Le Nouvelliste* 2023, January 4; Charles 2023, January 9; Janetsky 2023, January 21; CBS News 2023, January 27; Espérance 2023, February 2; UN News Global 2022, December 21).

The *Rasanbleman Sosyalis pou yon Inisyativ Nasyonal tou Nèf* (Assembly of the People's Socialist Party for a New National Initiative) issued a "Deklarasyon Pati Rasin Kan Pèp La Sou Konjonkti Politik Peyi A" ("Declaration of the People's Party on the Political Conjuncture of the Country") that the current situation is not an isolated incident but has its roots in the socioeconomic system based on the exclusion and exploitation of the majority for the benefit of the dominant classes and foreign investors supported by the imperialist powers (Fils-Aimé and Chalmers 2023, April 28).[5]

The use of gangs or paramilitary organizations by state leaders to suppress their opponents and remain in power has been a constant in Haiti's history. As Leslie Péan argued, the assassination of Jean-Jacques Dessalines, Haiti's first president, in 1806, officially inaugurated what he called the recourse to organized criminality by heads of state who would use their monopoly over the use of force to suppress those who opposed their dictates. Faustin Soulouque, who proclaimed himself emperor and ruled from 1847–1859, organized a terror squad known as the *Zinglins* to suppress and kill his opponents (Péan 2000, 348–349). François Duvalier, who ruled from 1957–1971, created his terror apparatus known as the Volunteers of National Security (popularly known as the *Tontons Macoutes*)[6] and modeled after Soulouque's *Zinglins*. Duvalier's state-sponsored terrorism reached unprecedented heights and spared no one in his aim to consolidate power. Men, women, children, families from all classes, and even entire towns were subjected to the tyrannical and unpredictable violence of the regime (Dupuy 1989, 160–161). Michel-Rolph Trouillot (1986) put it well when he wrote that Duvalier's violence "did not seek the physical intervention of the State in the battlefield of politics; it aimed to create a void in that field to the benefit of the state. It wanted an end to that struggle for a lack of combatants in the sphere occupied by the totalitarian executive" (180).

Jean-Bertrand Aristide, the populist and former Liberation Theology priest, was elected president in 1990, took office in February 1991, and was overthrown by the Haitian army in September 1991, exiled, and returned to Haiti in October 1994 by a US-led multinational force to complete his first five-year term. Aristide abolished the Haitian army and replaced it with a new Haitian National Police that was equipped and trained by the United States, Canada, and France. Reelected in 2000 for a second and final five-year term, Aristide, though still espousing a left-of-center, social democratic agenda, was now opposed by the progressive political parties that had supported him in 1990 as well as by the Haitian bourgeoisie. Relying only on his mass base for support, he deployed armed gangs to attack and kill members of the opposition and suppress demonstrations. The gangs, who came to be known as *chimères*, also acted autonomously, turned their neighborhoods into fiefs under their control, and engaged in drug trafficking and other criminal activities (Dupuy 2007, 144–145). As Robert Fatton (2002) put it, "having begun as a mere political instrument in the struggle for power, the *chimères* [became] a power unto themselves" (148). And some of the gangs operating in Port-au-Prince currently are allegedly linked to Aristide's former political party *Fanmi Lavalas* (Hjelmgaard and Beard 2023, March 11). Former president Michel Martelly (2011–2016) reportedly had ties to drug dealers, money launderers, and gang leaders, as did President Moïse, who allegedly recruited the leader of the G-9 Family and allied gangs that are now operating autonomously and terrorizing the population under what remains of the dysfunctional de facto Henry government (Ioanes 2023; Espérance 2023, July 4).

The question, then, is where does Haiti go from here? In response to the constitutional crisis created by the assassination of President Moïse, a coalition of civil society groups, labor unions, professional associations, human rights organizations, farmers' alliances, religious groups, and political organizations representing a large cross-section of the Haitian population formed a Commission for Haitian Solution to the Crisis. In August 2021 that Commission issued what came to be known as the Montana Accord after the hotel in Pétion-Ville where it was ratified (Commission 2021, August 9). The Accord called on the United States to compel Henry to step down on February 7, 2022, the date Moïse's term as president ended, and be replaced by a two-year representative transitional government that would address the basic needs of Haitians and organize free, fair, and participatory elections.

Going further than the 2019 agreement, the Accord called for an end to the "Anti-National State" that for the past two centuries has been subjected to the dictates of foreign powers for their benefit and those of local actors allied with them, and the creation of a new State that will respond to and serve the general interest. As such it considers that the right to life, liberty, human rights, equal access to opportunities, co-ownership of the wealth of the nation, and equal participation in deciding the agenda are fundamental and inalienable.

To that end, the Accord proposed the formation of a two-year transitional bicameral government comprised of members chosen by the organizations that represent the various sectors of the population, such as the peasantry, women, human rights, professionals, the State University, the private sector, religious institutions, labor unions, political organizations, and Haitians living abroad. Their priority would be to mobilize the citizenry; restore the regular functions of the state and juridical institutions; reinforce the public administration; create a climate of peace and security to guarantee, protect, and enforce human rights; and organize and hold national elections. Equally as important, to restore public trust in the institutions of government, all those who have engaged in corruption and the spoliation of public funds would need to be brought to justice to account for their crimes (Ibid.).

Prime Minister Henry is still in power and shows no sign of giving it up. He made that clear in his address to the country on February 7, 2022, the day his term in office ended, basically saying that the international community, by which he meant the core group of countries that decide Haitian affairs (United States, Canada, France) and the international financial institutions (IMF, World Bank, and Inter-American Development Bank), was behind him. He dismissed the Montana Accord's demand to form a transitional government on the ground that the constitution does not provide a legal mechanism to choose an interim president, adding that only elections could resolve the political impasse and that "no one has the authority or the right to meet at a hotel or abroad to decide in small committees who to be president or prime minister" (Thomas and Elsworth 2022). But neither does the constitution allow for a de facto prime minister to rule by decree. New parliamentary elections were not held in October 2019, and the term of its last remaining 10 senators ended on January 10, 2023 (Charles 2023, January 9). Henry also dissolved members of the provisional council in charge of organizing new legislative and presidential elections that were supposed to be held on November 7, 2022, but were postponed.

Ultimately it is the United States and Canada that will decide what happens, and the Biden administration and that of Canadian prime minister Justin Trudeau made it clear that they would continue to support Henry (Abi-Habib and Kitroeff 2022). He requested a multinational force to help support the police to fight the gangs, and the United States and Canada are contemplating different options, including possible military intervention if the situation continues to deteriorate (Charles 2023, January 27). Volker Türk, the UN Human Rights Commissioner, also urged the international community "to help the Haitian authorities regain full control so this suffering can be stopped" (Coto and Sanon 2023). But the United States wants Haiti to "address its continued insecurity challenges," as does Canada, mindful of the previous interventions that failed to bring long-term stability and opting for now to leave it to Haitians to find a solution to this crisis (Lederer 2023).

In July 2023, the UN Security Council adopted a resolution urging the international community to support the Haitian National Police, including the possible deployment of a specialized force. Neither the United States nor Canada is considering doing so, mindful of the failures of their previous interventions that "left a bitter taste among the Haitian population" (France 24 2023). The top general of the Canadian army offered the excuse that Canada is already stretched by assisting Ukraine in its war with Russia and may not be able to lead a security mission to Haiti. The UN Security Council asked Secretary General Antonio Guterres to present a report that could include the recommendation for such a UN-led mission by mid-August 2023. Kenya offered to lead such a force, and despite concerns with its police force's human rights record, Guterres, the United States, and Canada welcomed it. The Bahamas also made a commitment to send personnel to support that mission if authorized by the United Nations, as did Jamaica (Ibid.; Charles 2023, July 30; Correla 2023; Taylor 2023; Reliefweb 2023).

As Alessandro Ford points out, however, such a multinational force will face fearsome opponents who are heavily armed and well-trained paramilitaries who are much more familiar with their terrain, and often operate in complicity with the security forces, many of whom live in gang-controlled neighborhoods and are paid off by them (Ford 2023). If the past is prologue, however, even if the international police forces succeeded in neutralizing the criminal gangs and restored some semblance of order, they will do nothing to change the socioeconomic and political structures that gave rise to them now and in the past. Given the long history of the major countries' support for dictators and compelling successive governments, including those elected democratically, to adopt policies that transformed Haiti into a supplier of the cheapest labor for foreign capital in the hemisphere, many members of civil society organizations oppose another military intervention. As Mario Joseph, managing attorney for the Bureau des avocats internationaux, put it in his letter to the Caribbean Community (CARICOM), an "international intervention would 'prop up the unconstitutional, corrupt and repressive de facto government and stifle legitimate dissent,'" adding that the last UN stabilization mission in Haiti (MINUSTAH as it was known) from 2004 to 2017 "set the stage for today's spectacular rebound of gang violence and left Haiti less democratic than when it arrived" (Smith 2023). One could also add the recent increase of the cholera epidemic introduced in Haiti by UN peacekeeping troops that occupied Haiti from 2004 to 2017. Similarly, Monique Clesca (2023), a member of the Montana Accord, pointed out that "Haiti does not need foreign troops to solve its problems, but it does need the United States and its partners to stop propping up a corrupt government aligned with criminal gangs." Jacques Ted Saint-Dic, also a member of the Accord, noted that "if the country is offered adequate technical assistance, and if we are allowed to purchase arms and munitions, to conduct a certification and depoliticization process inside the Haitian National Police, and to sever the ties between the state and the gangs, we can put an end to the country's security crisis" (Johnston and François 2023).

Canada sent airplanes and ships designed to gather intelligence, surveillance, and reconnaissance to help the Haitian police in their fight against the gangs, and the United States supplied the police with sophisticated equipment (night vision goggles, advanced combat telescopic rifle scopes, riot helmets, ballistic vests) along with the armored vehicles that were purchased by the Haitian government (Lee 2023, February 5; Charles 2023, February 8). Knowing that he still has the support of the major powers, Henry formed his own Haut Conseil de Transition (HCT—High Transitional Council) to create the conditions for new presidential and parliamentary elections in 2023, which will be organized and supervised by an independent Provisional Electoral Council (Conseil Électoral Provisoire [CEP]) (Vant Bèf Info 2022). Fritz Jean, the president of the Montana Accord, decried those from the political, social, and economic sectors who aligned themselves with the Transitional Council to hold elections that will allow those in power to "maintain it and continue to control the most important institutions of the country" (Jean 2023). Most of its supporters, Clesca (2022) points out, "represent groups already aligned with Henry's government and benefiting from and invested in the corruption of the ruling class." Mark Schneider made a similar point: "Unless the Biden administration tells Henry that he has to step down or give up significant power to a broad coalition, including Montana group leaders . . . international resolutions demanding changes are near useless" (Schneider 2023).

In the midst of this political jostling, Father Tom Hagan, an American Roman Catholic priest who has been working with the people who live in Cité

Soleil, one of the largest shantytowns in Port-au-Prince, attempted what he called a fragile agreement with the rival gang leaders for a ceasefire (Charles 2023, July 14; Alphonse 2023, July 17). That effort did not last. The kidnappings and killings rebounded. Subsequently the US State Department ordered all nonemergency personnel at its embassy in Port-au-Prince and US citizens to leave Haiti (Charles 2023, July 30; Human Rights Watch 2023). As urgent as it may be to silence the gangs, however, the root cause of their existence lies in the socioeconomic conditions that compel individuals to resort to criminality as a way of life. Louis-Henri Mars made that point succinctly in response to the call for an international military force to neutralize the gangs: "You can go into the hoods with Swat teams and crack down on the gangs, but is there a plan for the day after? I have not seen one" (Daniels 2023). In that same vein, Monique Clesca put it well when she said:

> Haiti does not need a foreign military intervention.... Granted, the Haitian National police needs assistance to subdue the gangs and re-establish security. But a Kenyan or other foreign-led force would only serve to prop up Ariel Henry's failed government.... Haiti urgently needs the United States and its partners to stop supporting a corrupt government and to pressure it to reach a political accord with opposition and civil society, including the Montana Accord leaders, to have a transition that can address the catastrophic humanitarian situation, the calamitous security situation, stable and sustainable democratic state—that serves its people by fulfilling their basic human rights and follows the rule of law. (Latin American Advisor 2023)

In mid-August, and under the protection of the US State Department, a Kenyan delegation went to Haiti to meet with Haitian government officials and Prime Minister Henry's High Council of Transition to consider the possible deployment of a multinational force to work with the Haitian National Police to suppress the gangs and restore order in the country. The objective of the Kenyan force would not be to engage in confronting and suppressing the gangs, but to protect key government infrastructures such as the airport, seaports, and main roads, and leave that task to the Haitian police (Charles 2023, August 24).

On Monday, October 2, 2023, and with the full backing of the United States which pledged to contribute up to $200 million help finance it, the 15-member United Nations Security Council—with China and Russia abstaining—approved sending such a mission to Haiti. If Kenya's High Court approves the deployment of its police force, and if it is supplemented by additional forces from Jamaica, the Bahamas, and Antigua and Barbuda, they could be deployed in two or three months or early in 2024 (Coto 2023, October 2; Shuldiner 2023, October 4; Nation Africa 2023, October 10).

If successful, this objective would be in keeping with the demands of the Montana Accord. It remains to be seen, however, if such an intervention will also lead to elections that result in the formation of a democratic order that prioritizes the interests and the needs of the majority. This will be determined by the balance of class forces in the coming months and the respect of the will of that majority by the imperialist powers, notably the United States in the last instance.

II

The recent political crisis has also worsened the precarious needs of most of the population for more security, jobs, and better living conditions. For many, the only alternative was to leave Haiti and seek better opportunities abroad. In late September 2021, some 15,000 migrants, most of whom were Haitians, crossed the Mexican border into the Texas town of Del Rio. Of those, the US government returned some 5,500 to Haiti. Eight thousand returned to Mexico, and the remainder were put in removal proceedings that would determine if they can stay in the United States or be returned to Haiti. The decision by the Biden administration to return the migrants to Haiti led Daniel Foote, the administration's special envoy dealing with this crisis, to resign over the inhumane treatment they received in Texas as well as the decision to deport them (Biakolo 2022). In November 2021 the US Coast Guard intercepted some 700 migrants who tried to reach the coast of Florida and returned them to Haiti, and Cuba did the same for another 1,300 at the end of that year (Charles and Maxineau 2022). Still, the exodus continued, as did the interceptions and repatriations (Goodhue and Charles 2023). In November 2022, the Department of Homeland Security (DHS) extended the Temporary Protected Status (TPS) for Haiti through August 2024 for those who meet all eligibility requirements but excluded those who entered the United States illegally after November 6, 2022 (Charles 2021, September 10).

The recent arrivals in the United States migrated from various countries in South America where many had gone after the devastating 7.0 magnitude earthquake on January 12, 2010, that killed some 230,000; injured more than 300,000; and destroyed 250,000 homes and 35,000 commercial, industrial, and administrative buildings (Caroit 2010). But in most of those countries, such as Chile and Brazil, many faced hostilities and discrimination, and unable to regularize their status and find jobs or were expelled, they decided to make their way to the United States, where they believed they would have better opportunities as did those who came before them.

Responding to the emigration crisis, de facto Prime Minister Henry said during his address to the UN General Assembly on September 25, 2021, that this situation was caused by global inequality and that "migrations will continue as long as there are pockets of wealth on the planet, while the majority of the world population lives in precarity" (Peltz 2021). Inequality certainly plays its part in fueling emigration, but only in specific contexts that Prime Minister Henry did not spell out. Since it became independent from France in 1804 after its successful anticolonial slave revolution, Haiti remained a stratified and unequal society. Yet it was not until the twentieth century, and more specifically since the US occupation of Haiti from 1915 to 1934, that emigration became a permanent and determining feature of Haitian society.

It is estimated that in 2020 some 2,000,000 Haitians, or 19 percent of the population of 11 million, lived abroad. Of them, 705,000 live in the United States, 496,000 in the Dominican Republic, 237,000 in Chile, 343,000 in Brazil, 101,000 in Canada, 85,000 in France, 34,000 in Guadeloupe, 30,000 in the Bahamas, 22,000 in French Guiana, and 16,000 in Turks and Caicos (Yates 2021).

Natural disasters, such as the 2010 earthquakes mentioned above, and the more recent 7.2 magnitude quake in August 2021, which killed more than 2,000 people, injured 12,500, and displaced an estimated 800,000, played their part (UN News Global 2022, February 16). Likewise, political repression, such as during the 29-year Duvalier dictatorships from 1957–1986, and the overthrow of the populist president Jean-Bertrand Aristide by the Haitian army in September 1991, seven months after he took office, and again in February 2004 after serving only three of his second five-year terms, compelled tens of thousands to leave. And as outlined above, more recently the country has once again been mired in violence and insecurity with conflicts among rival gangs that are looting businesses, kidnapping people for ransom, and killing thousands, since the assassination of President Moïse in July 2021.

Important as these factors are in spurring emigration, I argue that they can be understood better in the broader context of the political economy of contemporary Haiti. By this I mean a capitalist economy where those who do not own property are compelled to sell their labor power, that is, their ability to work and produce commodities or render services for profit to the owners of properties or businesses and receive a wage or a salary in return.

Large-scale emigration from Haiti is a twentieth-century phenomenon. Throughout the nineteenth century when most Haitians lived in the countryside rather than in urban centers, and were engaged in agricultural labor, either as landowners, tenant farmers, or as day laborers to produce crops for sale in the domestic markets or for export, emigration, in contrast to migration to different regions of the country, did not play any role in the dynamics of the economy.

All that began to change during the US occupation of 1915–1934. As Alejandro Portes and John Walton argued, sustained labor emigration from the less developed to the more developed economies of the capitalist world system resulted from the penetration and transformation of the former by the later, such that the dominant classes in the less developed economies found it advantageous to release that labor, especially when the emigrants bore the risks and the costs of their migration (Portes and Walton 1981, 30). One of the objectives of the occupation was to facilitate the investment of US capital and the exploitation of both Haiti's natural resources and its labor. To make the former possible, the United States imposed a new constitution that for the first time since Haiti became independent allowed foreigners who were not married to Haitians to buy and own property. It created a centralized public administration; expanded technical education; and developed a modern infrastructure of roads, ports, railroads, and other transportation and communication networks to facilitate capital investments and the production and export of goods and raw materials to the new US businesses, which were established in sectors such as electricity, port and railroad construction, mining, banking, and large-scale plantation production such as pineapple, mangoes, sisal, bauxite, and sugar. The Haitian gourde was henceforth pegged to the US dollar rather than the French franc, and the United States became the single most important market for Haitian exports and imports.

All these enterprises could operate only if they had a labor force at their disposal. This was made possible by expropriating the lands of hundreds of thousands of farmers and transforming them into wage laborers, thereby accomplishing in short order what the Haitian bourgeoisie had not been able or needed to do for over 100 years, namely, expropriate the small landowners/possessors to create a proletariat they could employ in large plantations (see Chapter One). The proletarianization of Haitian peasants during the Occupation was not limited to supplying a labor force for the businesses operating in Haiti only. Tens of thousands of Haitians were sent to work on US-owned sugar and other agricultural plantations in Cuba and the Dominican Republic. But whereas Haitian emigration to Cuba ended in 1937, it continues unabated not only to the Dominican Republic but to other parts of the Caribbean, Central and South America, the United States, Canada, and France, as mentioned above.

Once unleashed, the proletarianization process continued after the occupation. In the 1930s, 1940s and 1950s, foreign companies came to Haiti to produce bananas, sugar, and rubber and to mine copper and bauxite for export. And since the 1970s, the United States, through the US Agency for International Development (USAID), the World Bank, and the Inter-American Development Bank, championed the export assembly industries as Haiti's main development strategy. Foreign investors were attracted to Haiti for a number of reasons: its abundant supply of unskilled, low-wage workers kept in check with violent repression and large numbers of unemployed workers to recruit; its close proximity to the US market; its lack of foreign exchange controls and other government interference; its policies allowing the free circulation of the US dollar; its tax incentives with exemptions on income and profits; and its tariff exemptions on imported raw materials, machinery, or other inputs used in the assembly industries, as well as on the export of their products (Dupuy 1997, esp. Ch. 2).

Although Port-au-Prince was and remains the epicenter of that industry in Haiti, it has subsequently expanded to other parts of the country. In the early 2000s, the World Bank and the Inter-American Development Bank helped finance the creation of free-trade zones in the northeast region of Haiti near the border with the Dominican Republic. Doing so required the eviction of thousands of peasant farmers in the fertile regions near the border and the appropriation of more than a thousand acres of their farms to build an industrial park, a power plant, and a deepwater port to support the park.

The United States and the international financial institutions continued to recommend the same policies after the devastating earthquake that shook Haiti in 2010. In response to it, the United States devised its Haiti Economic Lift Program (HELP), which extended the trade benefits of the 2006 Haiti Hemispheric Opportunity through Partnership Encouragement Act (HOPE) designed to boost clothing exports by offering tariff preferences and expanding duty-free exemptions for textile and apparel products (Steckley and Shamsie 2015).

Another major factor that fueled emigration was the accelerated decline of the agricultural sector under the Duvalier dictatorships from 1957 to 1986 when it turned over the formulation of economic policy to the World Bank, the IMF, and the Inter-American Development Bank. The policies they devised—such as reductions in protective tariffs and trade restrictions, tax incentives to investors, privatization of public enterprises, reduction of public spending and in public sector employment—had the net effect of not only transforming Haiti's near self-sufficiency in food production, but also into a supplier of the cheapest labor in the Western Hemisphere for the assembly industries.

Fifty percent of the population is employed in the agricultural sector, which generates one quarter of Haiti's gross domestic product. Up to the 1990s, Haiti produced all the rice it consumed and 80 percent of its foods. By the early 2000s, after the free-trade and structural adjustment policies the international financial institutions imposed that included tariff exemptions on food imports, Haiti produced only 42 percent of its foods and imported 80 percent of its rice, making it the fourth largest importer of subsidized US rice in the world.

The result of these policies was to reduce the earnings of the farmers employed in the agricultural sector and limit their ability to make productive investments in their farms, and the migration of many to urban centers or emigration to other countries in search of employment. Another factor that prevents farmers from improving their farms is the high cost of credit. On average, farmers own about two acres of land. Thirty-seven percent of the 64 percent of farmers who are indebted carry a debt burden that is equivalent to between 2 and 12 months of income, and 23 percent have burdens that are more than a year's worth of income (World Bank Group 2019, 1–2).

In addition, because of rising inflation, 8 out of 10 people are cutting back on meals, and farmers are compelled to reduce food production due to the rising cost of inputs such as seeds and fertilizers, reducing the purchasing power of the most vulnerable even more. Consequently, the average price of rice has increased by 59 percent, milk by 53 percent, and oil by 77 percent, and the cost of transportation has doubled. Food and transportation represent more than 65 percent of the average poor family's budget. It is estimated that currently 5 million people, or nearly half the population of 11 million, are struggling to feed themselves (World Food Program 2023; Charles 2023, June 16).

Conditions are not much better in urban areas. Contrary to the proponents of the assembly industry, it did not contribute to solving the chronic unemployment problem, which currently stands at 40 percent. But neither was it meant to do so. That industry was attracted to Haiti because its high rate of unemployment made it possible to hire workers who could be paid the lowest wages than anywhere else in the region. As I pointed out in Chapter One, in 2019, that industry employed 60,000 workers, with women comprising 68 percent of that labor force who are paid 32 percent less than men for doing the same work, all other things being equal. In November of that year, the Moïse government raised the minimum wage for workers in the assembly industry to $5.10 for an eight-hour day. The workers' unions demanded a minimum of $15/day to cover their basic needs. They went on strike again to press their demands, and in February 2022 the Henry government agreed to a 54 percent increase to $7.50/day, or half of what they sought (Mélodie 103.3 FM, 2022, Mar 2).

Even with such comparatively low wages, however, the current climate of insecurity is affecting the assembly industry and threatening its continued operation in the country. Recently, one of the largest employers in that sector, the Sae-A Trading Co., a Korean textile company that has been operating in Haiti for over a decade and was one of the largest investors in that sector, is closing one of its factories that employed some 1,000 workers. It plans on reducing the number of employees in its factories to 3,500 from 7,000. In all, since after the 2010 earthquake, the number of garment jobs in Haiti has declined from 60,000 to 49,000. Sectors other than apparel production are also affected by the deteriorating security environment, generating more layoffs and spurring more emigration. The head of the Association of Haitian

Industries acknowledged that fact when he said that "our nation's difficult socioeconomic challenges are worsening, putting thousands more out of work, and fueling migration" (Charles 2023, February 2).

Given these conditions, both in the rural and urban areas, and the relatively high surplus and unemployed labor they generate, it is not surprising that emigration is seen by many as the only alternative. Their desperation was reflected in a survey of the population conducted in October 2021 in which 82.4 percent said they would like to leave the country (*Le Nouvelliste* 2021, January 27). Moreover, emigration has become an imperative and a lifeblood for the families left behind and for the Haitian economy at large. Sixty-nine percent of families in Haiti now rely on remittances from emigrants to keep them afloat, and the transfers account for 25 percent of Haiti's gross domestic product and nearly twice as much as the combined value of its exports and foreign direct investment.

It is clear, then, that inequalities fuel emigration. But this is so only if one understands these inequalities as the product of Haiti's class relations, the transformation of its economic structures, and the functions it performs in the international division of labor of the capitalist world economy. In short, given that the Haitian bourgeoisie and successive governments capitulated to the demands of foreign and domestic capital for a compliant and low-paid labor force to maintain the country's "comparative advantage" in the region, exporting its surplus labor and relying on their remittances have become the *conditio sine qua non* of its participation in the world economy.

To mitigate this inevitable process of emigration, Alfred Pierre proposed an increase in the minimum wage as one of the measures that the government could pursue. He called on the government and employers to prove that doing so would have a negative impact on the rate of employment instead of serving the general interest insofar as it would not favor the interests of capital over those of labor. As he put it, "given that the question of the minimum wage is a choice and a political commitment to reduce social inequalities, the State would be justified in deciding in favor of workers as a means of reducing poverty" (Pierre 2017, August 22).

As I have argued, however, there is not and cannot be a "general interest" in a capitalist society. In such a society the principal objective of the capitalist is to produce commodities or services that create surplus value (profits) for their business. The precondition for the continual and expanded production of profit and the accumulation of capital is the commodification of all the means and factors of production, and the production of commodities for sale in national and world markets. But only labor can produce surplus value or profit. Once separated from or unable to control the means of production and providing for their and their families' livelihoods (e.g., farmers who own/possess land, shop/small business owners, market vendors), workers are compelled to sell their labor power in a market to capitalists in return for wages, and only by getting them to produce commodities that embody more value than they receive in the form of wages can the capitalists make a profit. Thus, the capitalists and the workers are locked in an inevitable and never-ending struggle. The objective of the former is to maximize profits by getting the workers to produce more each working day while keeping wages constant or even lowering them where possible, whereas the latter seek to increase wages without having to work or produce more. This sometimes leads to an impasse between them, often compelling the state/government to intervene to resolve the standoff, usually in favor of the employers as happened in the assembly industry when the government forced the workers to settle for half of what they demanded.

Capitalism is an inherently conflictual system. Whereas in any given working day/week/month/year those who own the means of production seek to extract the maximum profits from their employees without having to pay them more, the latter seek to increase their earnings (wages/salaries) without having to work or produce more. Creating a more just and more equal society in Haiti, then, will require far greater transformations than wage increases. Thomas Piketty (2020) put it well when he argued that only the state can ensure that everyone has access to the "fundamental goods, foremost among which are health, education, employment, the wage relation, and deferred wages for the elderly and unemployed. The goal should be to transform the entire distribution of income and wealth and, beyond that, the distribution of power and opportunities" (1003). Immanuel Wallerstein (2003) also made a similar point: "democracy is about equality. Without equality in all arenas of social life, there is no possible equality in any arena of social life, only the mirage of it. Liberty does not exist where equality is absent, since the powerful will always tend to prevail in an inegalitarian system" (166).

As I have shown, the emigration of Haitian labor, skilled and unskilled, is determined first and foremost by the social, political, and economic conditions in Haiti rather than on the immigration policies and the socio-economic conditions in those countries to which they emigrate, legally or illegally, and where they may or may not find the opportunities to create a better life for themselves and their families. The slaves of Saint-Domingue, who rebelled against their colonial and domestic masters, did so to create a new society that would accord with their interests. They succeeded in doing so to a large extent in the nineteenth century by controlling their own means of production and consumption and preventing the dominant classes from expropriating and proletarianizing them to recreate the plantation system of the colonial era. Even those who rented their land still controlled their means of production, their labor, and the products of their labor. As such, labor migration to urban centers or emigration did not configure in the dynamics of the society and the economy.

All that changed since the US occupation. The exodus will likely continue if large sectors of the rural population are compelled to migrate to urban centers and where, unable to earn their living as wage laborers, they have no alternative but to seek to do so abroad. Moreover, as I pointed out, insofar as the remittances that Haitian emigrants send to Haiti are twice as much as the combined value of its commodity exports and foreign investments, exporting its labor is and will remain its most lucrative trade.

NOTES

1. These numbers do not include those who were acting or provisional presidents, council of ministers, heads of military or government executive committees, or chairmen of the government junta (Haiti).

2. Translated as Bald-Head Haitian Party, it was named after its founder and former president Michel Martelly, who is bald.

3. It refers to the practice of members of the bourgeoisie funding those who hold public office to do their bidding (Dupuy 1989, 98).

4. For the IMF, it's "business as usual" with Haiti. As reported in *Haïti en Marche* (Mélodie 103.3 FM, 2023), in June 2023 it approved a new Staff-Monitored Program (SMP) "aimed at maintaining the country's macroeconomic stability and sustaining the recent reforms that reinforce the economy's resilience," notwithstanding the fact that the current rate of unemployment is 40 percent, nearly half of the population of 11 million are struggling to feed themselves, and tens of thousands are emigrating,

legally or illegally, to earn a living elsewhere and send remittances to support members of their families who remain in Haiti. I discuss this process more fully below.

5. "Deklarasyon Pati Rasin Kan Pèp La Sou Konjonkti Politik Peyi A." *Rasanbleman Sosyalis pou yon Inisyativ Nasyonal tou Nèf*. Port-au-Prince, April 28, 2023. "Declaration of the People's Party on the Political Conjuncture of the Country," by the Assembly of the People's Socialist Party for a New National Initiative.

6. The term is derived from the folkloric figure of an old man with a straw bag with a shoulder strap, a bogeyman who scared children.

Bibliography

Archival Sources and Abbreviations

AN Archives Nationales, Paris, France.

AE Fond Affaires Étrangères

Série B

Haïti: AE/B/III/380, 450, 458 (1818–1868)

AE/B/III/380 *Loi qui déclare dette nationale l'indemnité de 150,000,000 de francs accordée à la France, pour la reconnaissance de l'Indépendance d'Haïti*, 25 Fevrier 1826.

AN Archives Nationales, Pierrefitte-sur-Seine, Paris, France.

AP Archives Privées

156 AP/(1)/18-38 (carrier); 40–53 (correspondence), Fonds Privés/Archives Privées: Archives De Mackau

AP/15/1/20. Comte de Chabrol. Comte de Chabrol au baron de Mackau, 17 avril 1825.

AP-1-20. *Ordonnance du Roi*, 17 avril 1825.

AP-1-120. *Extrait des articles additionnels secret du traité du 30 mai 1814.*

AP-1-20. de Mackau, baron. *Rapport à Son Excellence le Ministre de la Marine et des Colonies, de la Mission à Saint-Domingue de Mr. Le Baron de De Mackau.* 7 Juillet 1825.

AP-1-20. Boyer, Jean-Pierre. Boyer, au Baron de Mackau, 8 juillet 1825.

ANOM Archives Nationale d'Outre-Mer, Aix-en-Provence, France.

Fond des Colonies

Saint-Domingue: Série principale – Sous-série CC9A (1789–1850)

Mémoires, correspondances, rapports, documents divers concernant Saint-Domingue. Demandes de renseignements, instructions pour les commissaires du roi envoyé en mission, négociations diplomatiques. Affaire Rochambeau (Jean-Baptiste, Donatien de Vimeur, comte de), général, gouverneur de Saint-Domingue de 1790 à 1792 (1814-1850). CC9A 47 à 54.

CC9A-216 MIOM-34 *Article additionnel secret au traité conclu le 30 mai 1814 entre la France et la Grande Bretagne*, 24 juin 1814.

CC9A – 48. *Rapport de Dauxion-Lavaisse à Malouet*, 1814.

MAE Ministère des Affaires Étrangères, Paris, France.

(MAE-CP) Affaires Politiques/Correspondance Politique: Haïti 1816–1895. Vol. 1–11: 1816–1843.

MAE 47CP Haïti: v. 5, 1831–1832, *Le Télégraph*, 19 Juin 1831.

MAE 47CP Haïti: v. 7. Las Cases, Baron de. Lettre tout à fait pour l'histoire, 7 février 1838.

MAE 47CP Haïti: v. 8, *Ordonnance du Roi*, 30 Mai 1838.

BNF Bibliothèque Nationale de France.

Gallica Bibliothèque Numérique: gallica.bnf.fr

Dalloz, Désiré, Phillippe Dupin, J.-Elisabeth-Merthie, and Antoine Louis Marie Hennequin. *Consultation de MM. Dalloz, Delarange, Hennequin, Dupin jeune et autres jurisconsultes pour les anciens colons de Saint-Domingue*. Paris: Impremerie de Madame Veuve Agasse, 1829.

Dubroca, L. *La vie de Toussaint Louverture, Chefs des noirs insurgés de Saint-Dominge*. Paris: 1802.

DuTertre, R. P. *Histoire* Générale des Antilles *Habitées par les François, Tome II*. Paris: Thomas Iolly, 1667.

Esmangart, Charles. *La Vérité sur les Affaires d'Haïti*. Paris: Imprimerie de Carpentier-Mérucourt, 1833.

France. *Traité entre la France et les puissances alliées: conclu à Paris, le 20 Novembre 1815.*

Hilliard D'Auberteuil, Michel-René. *Considérations sur l'état présent de la colonie française de Saint-Domingue*, 2 vols. Paris: Grangé, 1776. Manioc: Bibliothèque Numerique Amazonie Plateau des Guyanes.

Janvier, Louis-Joseph. *Les Constitutions d'Haïti (1801-1885)*. Paris: C. Marpon et E. Flammarion, 1886.

Pièces officielles relatives aux négociations du gouvernement français avec le gouvernement Haïtien pour traiter de la formalité de la reconnaissance de l'indépendance d'Haïti, 1824.

Raimond, Julien. *Mémoire sur les causes des désastres de la colonie de Saint-Domingue*. Paris: Imprimerie du Cercle Social, 1793.

Vendryes, B. *De L'Indemnité de Saint-Domingue: considérée souls le rapport du droit des gens, du droit public des Français et de la dignité nationale*. Paris, 1839.

Wallez, Jean Baptiste Guislain. *Précis historique des négociations entre la France et Saint-Domingue*. Paris: Ponthieu, 1826.

CIAT Centre Interministériel d'Aménagement du Territoire, Port-au-Prince, Haiti.

Ministère des Finances. État Détaillé des Liquidations opérées pendant l'année 1832 et les six premiers mois de 1833. Paris: Imprimerie Royale, 1834.

FCO Foreign Office and Commonwealth Office Collection (1816), No. 14, 38–39. Pétion. Pièces relatives à la correspondence de MM. les Commissaires de S. M. Très-Chrétienne et du Président d'Haïti. University of Manchester, John Ryland University Library. Accessed February 20, 2014. Http://www.jstor.org/stable/60234976.

The National Archives, Kew, Richmond, England.

Haiti and President (1807–1818): Pétion. *Piéces relatives à la correspondence de MM. les Commisaires de S. M. Très-Chrétienne et du Président d'Haïti*. University of

Manchester, John Ryland University Library. Accessed February 20, 2014. http://www.jstor.org/stable/60234976.

University of Florida, Gainseville, Florida.

Rochambeau Papers.

Gambart. *Observations présentées au gouvernement sur l'administration générale de Saint-Domingue*, 27 Mars 1802.

Idlinger, Joseph Antoine. *Rapport sur la 4e question qui m'à été faite aujourd'hui par le citoyen général en chef conçue en ces termes*. 3 Avril 1802.

USI Inquiry into Occupation and Administration of Haiti and Santo Domingo.

Hearing Before a Select Committee on Haiti and Santo Domingo, United States Senate, 67th Congress, First Session, August 5, 1921.

SECONDARY SOURCES

Abi-Habib, Maria. "Haiti's Leader Kept a List of Drug Traffickers. His Assassins Came for It." *The New York Times*, December 12, 2021. https://www.nytimes.com/2021/12/12/world/americas/jovenel-moise-haiti-president-drug-traffickers.html/.

Abi-Habib, Maria, and Natalie Kitroeff. "Haiti Opposition Group Calls on U.S. to End Support for Current Government." *The New York Times*, February 6, 2022. https://web.archive.org/web/20230714093831/https://www.nytimes.com/2022/02/06/world/americas/haiti-opposition-group-montana-accord.html.

Adam, André Georges. *Une crise haïtienne 1867-1869: Sylvain Salnave*. Port-au-Prince: Henri Deschamps, 1982.

Adeeko, Adeleke. *The slave's rebellion: Literature, history, orature*. Bloomington, IN: Indiana University Press, 2005.

Al Jazeera. "Haiti 'Dangling over an Abyss,' UN Human Rights Chief Says." May 3, 2023. https://www.aljazeera.com/news/2023/5/3/haiti-dangling-over-an-abyss-un-human-rights-chief-says.

———. "United Nations Statistics Underscore 'Extreme Brutality' of Haiti's Gangs." August 19, 2023. https://www.aljazeera.com/news/2023/8/19/united-nations-statistics-underscore-extreme-brutality-of-haitis-gangs.

BIBLIOGRAPHY

Alphonse, Roberson. "De la trêve des gangs de Cité Soleil." *Le Nouvelliste*. 17 juillet 2023. https://www.lenouvelliste.com/article/243432/de-la-treve-des-gangs-de-cite-soleil.

———. "Accalmie ou miroir aux alouettes?" *Le Nouvelliste* 20 juillet 2023. http://www.lenouvelliste.com/en/article/243506/accalmie-ou-miroir-aux-alouettes.

Anderson, Jon Lee. "Haiti Held Hostage." *The New Yorker*, July 17, 2023. https://www.newyorker.com/magazine/2023/07/24/haiti-held-hostage.

Anderson, Perry. "Modernity and Revolution." *New Left Review* 144 (March–April 1984): 96–113.

Anglade, Mireille Neptune. *L'autre moitié du développement: à propos du travail des femmes en Haïti*. Pétion-Ville: Éditions des Alizés, 1986.

Anievas, Alexander, and Kerem Nisancioglu. *How the West Came to Rule: The Geopolitical Origins of Capitalism*. London: Pluto Press, 2015.

Ardouin, Beaubrun. Études sur *l'Histoire d'Haïti*. 11 vols. 1853–1860. Port-au-Prince: F. Dalencourt, 1958.

Aristide, Jean-Bertrand. "Discours de Son Excellence Jean-Bertrand Aristide, Président de la République, à l'occasion de la Cérémonie Commémorative du Bicentenaire de la Mort de Toussaint Louverture." Port-au-Prince: Musée du Panthéon National, 7 avril 2003.

Arrighi, Giovanni. *Adam Smith in Beijing: Lineages of the Twentieth Century*. London: Verso, 2001.

Auguste, Claude B., and Marcel B. Auguste. *L'expédition Leclerc 1801-1803*. Port-au-Prince: Henri Deschamps, 1985.

Ayti Kale Je/Haiti Grassroots Watch. "Anti-Union, Pro 'Race to the Bottom,'" 2011. http://haitigrassrootswatch.squarespace.com/11_2_eng.

Barros, Jacques. *Haiti de 1804 à nos jours*. 2 vols. Paris: Éditions l'Harmattan, 1984.

Beauvois, Frédérique. "L'indemnité de Saint-Domingue: 'Dette d'independence' ou 'rançon de l'esclavage'?" *French Colonial History* 10 (2009): 109–124.

Beckert, Sven. *Empire of Cotton: A Global History*. New York: Alfred A. Knopf, 2014.

Behrendt, Stephen D., David Eltis, and David Richardson. "The Costs of Coercion: African Agency in the Pre-Modern Atlantic World." *The Economic History Review* 54, no. 3 (August 2001): 454–476.

Bell, Beverly. *Walking on Fire: Haitian Women's Stories of Survival and Resistance.* Ithaca: Cornell University Press, 2001.

———. "Women Farmers and Land Grabs in Haiti: An Interview with Iderle Brénus." Food First. Published February 18, 2016. https://web.archive.org/web/20220119022651/https://foodfirst.org/women-farmers-and-land-grabs-in-haiti-an-interview-with-iderle-brenus/.

Bell, Beverly, and Alexis Erket. "Garment Assembly Workers in Caracol, Haiti's Newest Free Trade Zone." Other Worlds. Published April 25, 2013.

Bellande, Alex, et al. *Espace rural et société agraire en transformation: des jardins haïtien aux marchés de Port-au-Prince.* Port-au-Prince: Institut Français d'Haïti, 1980.

Bellegarde, Dantès. *La nation haïtienne.* Paris: J. De Gigord, 1938.

Biakolo, Kovie. "The Black Migrant Trail of Tragedies." *The Nation*, February 8, 2022. https://www.thenation.com/article/society/black-migration-racism/.

Blackburn, Robin. *The American Crucible: Slavery, Emancipation and Human Rights.* London: Verso, 2011.

Blaise, Juhakenson. "Report: Kidnappings and Killings Resume in Haiti, Ending "Bwa Kale" Reprieve." *The Haitian Times*, July 17, 2023. http://haitiantimes.com/2023/07/17/report-kidnappings-and-killings-resume-in-haiti-ending-bwa-kale-reprieve/.

Blancpain, François. *Un ciècle de relations financières entre Haïti et la France (1825–1922).* Paris: L'Harmattan, 2001.

Bogues, Anthony. *Empire of Liberty: Power, Desire, and Freedom.* Hanover and London: University Press of New England, 2010.

Bonaparte, Napoléon. *Correspondance de Napoléon Ier. Tome Septième.* Paris: Henri Plon and J. Dumaine, 1861.

———. *Napoleon's Autobiography.* The Personal Memoirs of Bonaparte Compiled from his own Letters and Diaries by F. M. Kircheisen. Translated by Frederick

Collins. With an "Introduction" by Henry Irving Brock. New York: Duffield & Company, 1931.

———. *Napoleon's Memoirs*. Edited by Somerset de Chair. London: Faber and Faber Limited, 1946.

Boyer, Jean-Pierre. *Code Rural de Boyer 1826*. Port-au-Prince: Archives Nationales d'Haïti and Henri Deschamps, 1992.

Brière, Jean-François. *Haïti et la France 1804–1848: Le rêve brisé*. Paris: Editions Karthala, 2008.

Brenner, Robert. "The Origins of Capitalist Development: A Critique of Neo-Smithian Marxism." *New Left Review* 104 (1977): 25–92.

Brisson, Gérald. "Fondements économiques de la situation révolutionnaire en Haïti: 1945-1946 (Extraits)," 77–89, in *Trente ans de pouvoir en Haïti, 1: L'explosion de 1946: Bilan et perspectives*. Edited by Cary Hector, Claude Moïse, and Émile Olivier. Lasalle: Collectif Paroles, 1976.

Buck-Morss, Susan. *Hegel, Haiti, and Universal History*. Pittsburgh: University of Pittsburgh Press, 2009.

Buffaerts, Jean Claude. "Le cercle vicieux du surendettement." In *Haiti-France: Les chaînes de la dette. Le rapport Mackau (1825)*. Edited by Marcel Dorigny, Jean Marie Théodat, Gusti-klara Gaillard, and Jean Claude Buffaerts, 103–123. Paris: Maisonneuve & Larose, 2021.

Burnard, Trevor, and John Garrigus. *The Plantation Machine: Atlantic Capitalism in French Saint-Domingue and British Jamaica*. Philadelphia: University of Pennsylvania Press, 2016.

Cabon, Adolphe. *Histoire d'Haïti*, 4 vols. Paris: Congrégation des Frères de Saint-Jacques, 1929.

Caroit, Jean-Michel. "Comment la France a préparé son retour en Haiti: Le rapport du comité présidé par Regis Debray preconisait une concertation avec Washington." *Le Monde*, 15 avril 2004.

———. "René Preval: La Communauté international a confiance." *Le Monde*, 2 février 2010.

Casimir, Jean. *The Haitians: A Decolonial History*. Translated by Laurent Dubois. Chapel Hill: University of North Carolina Press, 2020.

Castor, Suzy. *L'occupation américaine d'Haïti*. Port-au-Prince: Imprimerie Deschamps, 1988.

CBS News. "Haitian Gangs' Gruesome Murders of Police Spark Protests as Calls Mount for Canada to Intervene." January 27, 2023. https://www.cbsnews.com/news/haiti-news-airport-protest-ariel-henry-gangs-murder-police/.

Célius, Carlo Avierl. "Le modèle social haïtien: Hypothèses, arguments et méthode." *Pouvoirs dans la Caraïbe*. Accessed October 15, 2015. http://plc.revues.org/738.

Central Intelligence Agency. *The World Fact Book*. Washington, DC: Central Intelligence Agency, 2019.

———. *The World Fact Book*. Washington, DC, June 10, 2020. https://www.cia.gov/the-world-factbook/.

Centre d'analyse et de recherche en droits de l'homme (CARDH). "Bwa kale": Deuxième Bilan Et Urgente Obligation De Proteger/Impact of the "Bwa Kale" Movement Over Insecurity and Kidnapping in Haiti/Impacts Du "Bwa Kale" Sur L'insécurité Et le Kidnapping en Haïti. March 7, 2023.

Césaire, Aimé. *Toussaint Louverture: La Révolution française et le problème colonial*. Paris: Livre Club Diderot, 1960.

Charles, Carolle. "Gender and Politics in Contemporary Haiti: The Duvalierist State, Transnationalism, and the Emergence of a New Feminism (1980-1990)." *Feminist Studies* 21, no. 1 (1995).

Charles, Jacqueline. "DHS Extends Temporary Protected Status for Haitians, Central Americans and Others." *Miami Herald*, September 10, 2021. https://www.miamiherald.com/news/nation-world/world/americas/haiti/article254123068.html.

———. "Made in Miami: How a South Florida Plot to Oust Haiti's Jovenel Moïse Led to His Murder." *Miami Herald*, December 8, 2022. https://www.miamiherald.com/news/nation-world/world/americas/haiti/article264470076.html.

———. "In Exclusive Interview, Haiti Prime Minister Says He'd Hand Assassination Suspects to U.S." *Miami Herald*, January 12, 2022. https://www.miamiherald.com/news/nation-world/world/americas/haiti/article258301873.html.

———. "How U.S. Sanctions Turn People into 'Economic Pariahs' and Why Some Call It a Civil Death." *Miami Herald*, January 5, 2023. https://www.miamiherald.com/news/nation-world/world/americas/haiti/article270036387.html.

———. "Armed Gangs Massacre Haitians and Torch Towns North of the Capital." *Miami Herald*, January 12, 2022. https://www.miamiherald.com/news/nation-world/world/americas/haiti/article269494152.html.

———. "With Not a Single Leader Left, Haiti Is Becoming a Textbook of a 'Failed State.'" *Miami Herald*, January 9, 2023. https://www.miamiherald.com/news/nation-world/world/americas/haiti/article270922407.html.

———. "Violence Erupts in Haiti during Protests by Police Officers after Gangs Killed Six Cops." *Miami Herald*, January 27, 2023. https://www.miamiherald.com/news/nation-world/world/americas/haiti/article271702052.html.

———. "Once the Promise of Hope in Haiti, Textile Park Is Now Laying Off Thousands of Workers." *Miami Herald*, February 2, 2023. https://www.miamiherald.com/news/nation-world/world/americas/haiti/article271963327.html.

———. "U.S. Is Training Haiti Police to Combat Gangs, But That's Not Its Only Security Worry." *Miami Herald*, February 8, 2023. https://www.miamiherald.com/news/nation-world/world/americas/haiti/article272244183.html.

———. "This U.S. Diplomat Went to Haiti to Talk Policing. Then He Got a Close Look at the Chaos." *Miami Herald*, February 8, 2023. https://www.miamiherald.com/news/nation-world/world/americas/haiti/article272062762.html.

———. "Canada Issues New Sanctions Against Haitians, Will Deploy Navy Ships Around Haiti Coast." *Miami Herald*, February 17, 2023. https://www.miamiherald.com/news/nation-world/world/americas/haiti/article272529821.html.

———. "Biden Official on Haiti: 'Incredibly Complex, Challenging.' Still No Respite in Sight." *Miami Herald*, February 23, 2023. https://miamiherald.com/news/nation-world/world/americas/haiti/article272582280.html.

———. "As Humanitarians Call for Greater Attention to Haiti, U.S. Pushes New Approach to Aid." *Miami Herald*, March 28, 2023. https://www.miamiherald.com/news/nation-world/world/americas/haiti/article273656000.html.

———. "After Cops Were Killed, Haiti Police Launched an Operation. Here's What Happened Next." *Miami Herald*, May 31, 2023. https://www.miamiherald.com/news/nation-world/world/americas/haiti/article275956881.html.

———. "Canada Slaps Sanctions on a Powerful Haiti Businessman and Gang Leaders." *Yahoo!* June 23, 2023. https://www.yahoo.com/entertainment/canada-slaps-sanctions-powerful-haitian-123656631.html.

———. "Record Hunger, Armed Gangs and Raging Inflation: U.N. Convenes Special Meeting on Haiti Crisis." *Miami Herald*, June 16, 2023. https://www.miamiherald.com/news/nation-world/world/americas/haiti/article276434826.html.

———. "With Help from American Priest, Four Haiti Gang Leaders Have Called a Truce. Can It Last?" *Miami Herald*, July 14, 2023. https://www.miamiherald.com/news/nation-world/world/americas/haiti/article277316038.html.

———. "Exclusive: Confidential U.N. Document Spells Out Thinking on Foreign Troops for Haiti." *Miami Herald*, July 26, 2023. https:///miamiherald.com/news/nation-world/world/americas/haiti/article277018333.html.

———. "'An Excellent Development,' Haiti Says of Kenya's Offer to Deploy 1,000 Police to Help." *Miami Herald*, July 30, 2023. https://miamiherald.com/news/nation-world/world/americas/haiti/article277792913.html.

———. "A U.S. Delegation Visited Kenya about Helping Haiti—and Was Surprised by the Response." *Miami Herald*, August 3, 2023. https://miamiherald.com/news/nation-world/world/americas/haiti/article277937608.html.

———. "U.N. Leader Offers Options for Tackling Haiti's Security Crisis. Goes Beyond Troops." *Miami Herald*, August 16, 2023. https://www.miamiherald.com/news/nation-world/world/americas/haiti/article278280563.html.

———. "On Eve of Kenya Delegation Visit to Haiti, Gang Violence Soars, Bodies Litter Streets." *Miami Herald*, August 19, 2023. https://www.miamiherald.com/news/nation-world/world/americas/haiti/article278382669.html.

———. "A Delegation from Kenya Leaves Haiti. Will Its Proposal Prove Effective Against Gangs?" *Miami Herald*, August 24, 2023. https://miamiherald.com/news/nation-world/world/americas/haiti/article278535869.html.

———. "How Dangerous Is Haiti? Still Too Risky to Retrieve Massacre Victims' Bodies." *Miami Herald*, August 28, 2023. https://miamiherald.com/news/nation-world/world/americas/haiti/article278679169.html.

Charles, Jacqueline, and David Goodhue. "Recent Arrivals of Hundreds of Haitians in the Keys Is a Sign of New Trafficking Routes." *Miami Herald*, March 11,

2022. https://www.miamiherald.com/news/nation-world/world/americas/haiti/article259285014.html.

Charles, Jacqueline, and Gérard Maxineau. "Coast Guard Has Returned to Haiti Most of the 356 Haitians Who Arrived in Keys This Week." *Miami Herald*, March 11, 2022. https://www.miamiherald.com/news/nation-world/world/americas/haiti/article259307034.html.

Charlmers, Camille, Guelsonne Calixte, François Gérard Junior Denart, Tonny Joseph, and Marc Cohen. "Can Haiti's Peanut Value Chain Survive US Generosity? Political Economy Analysis." PAPDA and OXFAM, 2020.

———. "Camille Charlmers plaide en faveur d'une augmentation significative de salaire minimum." *Le Nouvelliste*, 4 Avril 2019.

Chavla, Leah. "Haiti Research File: Bill Clinton's Heavy Hand on Haiti's Vulnerable Agricultural Economy: The American Rice Scandal." *Council on Hemispheric Affairs*, April 13, 2010. https://coha.org/haiti-research-file-neoliberalism%E2%80%99s-heavy-hand-on-haiti%E2%80%99s-vulnerable-agricultural-economy-the-american-rice-scandal/.

Cheney, Paul. *Cul de Sac: Patrimony, Capitalism, and Slavery in French Saint-Domingue*. Chicago: University of Chicago Press, 2017.

Clarkson, Thomas. *Henry Christophe and Thomas Clarkson: A Correspondence*. Edited by Earl Leslie Griggs and Clifford H. Prator. Berkeley and Los Angeles: University of California Press, 1952.

Clesca, Monique. "Haiti's Fight for Democracy: Why the Country Must Rebuild Before It Votes." *Foreign Affairs*, February 1, 2022. https://www.foreignaffairs.com/articles/haiti/2022-02-01/haitis-fight-democracy.

———. "Haiti's Rule of Lawlessness: Why a Military Intervention Would Only Entrench the Island's Problems." *Foreign Affairs*, March 10, 2023. https://www.foreignaffairs.com/central-america-caribbean/haitis-rule-lawlessness.

Code Henry. Cap Henry: Chez P. Roux, n.d.

Cole, Hubert. *Christophe, King of Haiti*. New York: Viking Press, 1967.

Collier, Paul. *Haiti: From Natural Catastrophe to Economic Security: A Report for the Secretary-General of the United Nations*. Oxford University: Department of Economics, 2009.

Comay, Rebecca. *Mourning Sickness: Hegel and the French Revolution*. Stanford: Stanford University Press, 2010.

Commission pour la Recherche d'une Solution Haïtienne á la Crise: Accord du 30 août 2021. August 9, 2021. https://crshc.ht/wp-content/uploads/sites/8/2021/09/accord-crshcht.pdf.

Coradin, Jean D. *Histoire Diplomatique d'Haïti 1804-1843*. Port-au-Prince: Edition des Antilles, 1988.

Corredor, Elizabeth S. "Unpacking 'Gender Ideology' and the Global Right's Antigender Countermovement." *Signs: Journal of Women in Culture and Society* 44, no. 3 (2019): 613–638.

Correla, Kinisha. "Bahamas to Deploy 150 Police Officers to Haiti amid Violence." Caribbean National Weekly.com. August 3, 2023. https://www.caribbeannationalweekly.com/news/caribbean-news/bahamas-to-deploy-150-police-officers-to-haiti-amid-violence/.

Coto, Danica. "UN Chief Insists on Deploying Special Forces as Crises in Haiti Worsen." *PBS News Hour*, January 23, 2023. pbs.org/newshour/world/un-chief-insists-on-deploying-special-armed-forces-as-crises-in-haiti-worsen.

Coto, Danica, and Evens Sanon. "UN Human Rights Chief Calls for Special Forces to Haiti." *AP News*, February 10, 2023. https://apnews.com/article/politics-brooklyn-united-nations-caribbean-haiti-4d32d1bfc05b0b9297914d228f79993f.

———. "UN Security Council Approves Sending a Kenya-led Force to Haiti to Fight Violent Gangs." *ABC News*, October 2, 2023. https://www.abcnews.go.com/international/wireStory/security-council-votes-send-kenya-led-multinational-force-103669296.

Cournand, Antoine de (Abbé). "Requête présentée à nosseigneurs de l'Assemblée Nationale en faveur *et l'abolition de l'esclavage. Vol 4: Traite des noirs et esclavage*. Paris: Éditions d'Histoire Sociale, 1968.

———. "des gens de couleur de l'île de Saint-Domingue, 1790." In *La Révolution française et l'abolition de l'esclavage. Vol 4:Traite des noirs et esclavage*. Paris: Éditions d'Histoire Sociale, 1968.

Curtin, Philip D. *Economic Change in Precolonial Africa: Senegambia in the Era of the Slave Trade*. Madison: University of Wisconsin Press, 1975.

Dartigue, Maurice. *Conditions Rurales en Haïti: Quelques donnés basées en partie sur l'étude de 884 familles.* Port-au-Prince: Imprimerie de l'état, 1938.

Daniels, Joe. "Haiti Political Deadlock Slows Push for International Force to Battle Gangs." *Financial Times*, July 17, 2023. https://www.ft.com/content/63f8107f-4a21-430b-aa5f-fa7f3b242f48.

Davis, David Brion. *The Problem of Slavery in the Age of Revolution 1770-1823.* Ithaca: Cornell University Press, 1975.

_____. *Inhuman Bondage: The Rise and Fall of Slavery in the New World.* Oxford and New York: Oxford University Press, 2006.

Dayan, Joan. *Haiti, History, and the Gods.* Berkeley and Los Angeles: University of California Press, 1995.

De Beauvoir, Simone. *The Second Sex.* Translated and edited by H. M. Parshley. New York: Vintage Books, 1974.

Debien, Gabriel. *Comptes, profits, esclaves, et travaux de deux sucreries de Saint-Domingue, 1774-1798*, 2 vols. Port-au-Prince: Imprimerie Valcin, 1945.

_____. "Gens de couleur et colons de St. Domingue." *Revue d'histoire de l'Amérique française*, no. 4, 1950.

_____. "Plantations et esclaves à Saint-Domingue: Sucrerie Cotineau, 1750-77." *Notes d'Histoire Coloniale* 66 (1962): 7–84.

Debray, Régis, et al. *Haïti et la France: Rapport à Dominique de Villepin, ministre des Affaires étrangères.* Paris: Éditions La Table Ronde, 2004.

De Hoog, Cius. *The Complicity of Women in Child Slavery: A Gender Analysis of Haiti and the Restavèk System.* Thesis submitted for the Degree of Philosophy in the University of Hull, East Riding, England, UK, 2017.

Delince, Kern. *Quelle armée pour Haïti?* Paris: Karthala, 1994.

Desmangles, Leslie. *The Faces of the Gods: Vodou and Roman Catholicism in Haiti.* Chapel Hill: University of North Carolina Press, 1992.

De Vaissière, Pierre. *Saint-Domingue: La Société et la Vie Créoles sous l' Ancien Régime (1629-1789).* Paris: Perrin, 1909.

D'Hondt, Jacques. "Le parcourt Hégélien de la Révolution française." *Bulletin de la Société française de philosophie* 83 (octobre-decembre 1989): 115–130.

Djaya, Dira, Drusilla Brown, and Luisa Lupo. "An Impact Evaluation of Better Work from a Gender Perspective: Analyzing Worker Surveys from Haiti, Nicaragua, Indonesia, Vietnam and Jordan." BetterWork. Published April 2019. https://betterwork.org/wp-content/uploads/Discussion-Paper-30.pdf.

Dobb, Maurice. "From Feudalism to Capitalism." In *The Transition from Feudalism to Capitalism: A Symposium*. Edited by Rodney H. Hilton, 165–169. London: New Left Book, 1976.

Dominican Today. "The Role of Women in Gangs in Haiti: From an Active Role to Simply Supporting the Partner." May 20, 2023. https://dominicantoday.com/dr/world/2023/05/20/the-role-of-women-in-gangs-in-haiti-from-an-active-role-to-simply-supporting-the-partner/.

Dorigny, Marcel. "De l'arrogance coloniale à la tentative d'intégration post-impériale 91804-1825)." In Marcel Dorigny, Jean-Marie Théodat, Gusti-Klara Gaillard, et Jean Claude Buffaerts, eds., *Haïti-France: Les chaînes de la dette: Le rapport Mackau (1825)*, 23–46. Paris, Maisonneuve & Larose, 2021.

Dorsinville, Luc. *Abregé d'histoire d'Haïti*. Port-au-Prince: Imprimerie de l'État, 1961.

Douglas, Paul H. "The Political History of the Occupation." In *Occupied Haiti*. Edited by Emily Green Balch, 15–36. New York: Writers Publishing Co., Inc., 1927.

DuBois, W. E. B. *The Souls of Black Folks*. New York and Scarborough, Ontario: The New American Library, 1969.

Dupuy, Alex. "Spanish Colonialism and the Origin of Underdevelopment in Haiti." *Latin American Perspectives* III, no. 2 (1976): 5–29.

———. *Feudalism and Slavery: Processes of Uneven Development in France and Saint-Domingue in the Eighteenth Century*. PhD Dissertation. Department of Sociology, State University of New York at Binghamton, 1981.

———. *Haiti in the World Economy: Class, Race, and Underdevelopment Since 1700*. Boulder: Westview Press, 1989.

———. *Haiti in the New World Order: The Limits of the Democratic Revolution*. Boulder: Westview Press, 1997.

———. "Globalization, the World Bank, and the Haitian Economy." In *Contemporary Caribbean Cultures and Societies in a Global Context*. Edited by

Franklin W. Knight and Teresita Martinez-Vergne, 43–70. Chapel Hill: University of North Carolina Press, 2005.

———. *The Prophet and Power: Jean-Bertrand Aristide, the International Community, and Haiti*. Lanham and Boulder: Rowman & Littlefield, Publishers, Inc., 2007.

———. "Disaster Capitalism to the Rescue: The International Community and Haiti after the Earthquake." *NACLA Reports on the Americas* 43, no. 4 (July/August 2010): 14–19.

———. "Jean-Bertrand Aristide's Return: Homecoming or Comeback?" *The Guardian*, Friday March 18, 2011. https://www.theguardian.com/commentisfree/cifamerica/2011/mar/18/haiti-jean-bertrand-aristide.

———. *Haiti: From Revolutionary Slaves to Powerless Citizens: Essays on the Politics and Economics of Underdevelopment, 1804-2013*. London and New York: Routledge, 2014.

———. *Rethinking the Haitian Revolution: Slavery, Independence, and the Struggle for Recognition*. Lanham: Rowman & Littlefield, 2019.

Dupuy, Alex, and Paul Fitzgerald. "A Contribution to the Critique of the World-System Perspective." *Insurgent Sociologist* Spring (1977): 113–124.

Duramy, Benedetta Faedi. *Gender and Violence in Haiti: Women's Path from Victims to Agents*. New Brunswick: Rutgers University Press, 2014.

Dye, Alan. *Cuban Sugar in the Age of Mass Production: Technology and the Economics of Sugar Central 1899-1929*. Stanford: Stanford University Press 1998.

Ebert, Teresa, L. *Ludic Feminism and After: Postmodernism, Desire, and Labor in Late Capitalism*. Ann Arbor: University of Michigan Press, 1999.

Engels, Frederick. *The Origin of the Family, Private Property and the State*. Edited by Eleanor Burke Leacock. New York: International Publishers, 1973.

———. "The Condition of the Working Class in England." In Karl Marx and Frederick Engels, *Collected Works*, Vol. 4. New York: International Publishers, 1975.

Enzenberger, Hans Magnus. "Las Casas, or a Look Back into the Future." In *The Devastation of the Indies: A Brief Account*. Bartolome de Las Casas. Translated from the Spanish by Herma Briffault. New York: Seabury Press, 1974.

Ehrenreich, Barbara. "What Is Socialist Feminism?" In *Materialist Feminism: A Reader in Class, Difference, and Women's Live.* Edited by Rosemary Hennessy and Chrys Ingraham, 69–70. New York and London: Routledge, 1997.

Espérance, Pierre. "Haiti's Police Protests Highlight Armed Gangs' Ties to Government." Just Security. February 2, 2023. https://www.justsecurity.org/84990/haitis-police-protests-highlight-armed-gangs-ties-to-government/.

———. "More Police Won't Solve Haiti's Crisis." *Foreign Policy*, July 4, 2023. https://foreignpolicy.com/2023/07/04/haiti-crisis-henry-police-gangs-security-politics-united-states/.

Etienne, Eddy. *La vraie dimension de la politique extérieure des premiers gouvernements d'Haïti (1804-1843)*. Québec: Editions Naaman, 1982.

Eugène, Itazienne. "La normalization des relation franco-haïtiennes (1825-1838)." In Marcel Dorigny, ed., *Haïti: première république noire*, 148–154. Paris: Publications de la Société Française d'Histoire d'Outre-Mer, et Association pour l'Étude de la Colonisation Europeenne, 2003.

Fanon, Frantz. *Black Skin, White Masks*. Translated from the French by Charles Lam Markmann. New York: Grove Press, 1967.

Farmer, Paul. "Douze points en faveur de la restitution à Haïti de la dette française." Institute for Justice & Democracy in Haiti. November 3, 2003. Accessed May 11, 2018.

Fatton, Robert, Jr. *Haiti's Predatory Republic: The Unending Transition to Democracy*. Boulder, CO: Lynne Rienner, 2002.

———. *The Roots of Haitian Despotism*. Boulder: Lynne Rienner Publishers, 2007.

———. *Haiti: Trapped in the Outer Periphery*. Boulder, CO: Lynne Rienner Publishers, Inc., 2014.

Fauvelet De Bourrienne, Louis Antoine. *Memoirs of Napoleon Bonaparte*. Edited by R. W. Phipps. New York: Charles Scribner's Sons, 1895.

Fick, Carolyn E. *The Making of Haiti: The Saint-Domingue Revolution from Below*. Knoxville: University of Tennessee Press, 1990.

———. "The French Revolution in Saint-Domingue: A Triumph or a Failure?" In *A Turbulent Time: The French Revolution and the Greater Caribbean*. Edited by

David Barry Gaspar and David Patrick, 51–75. Bloomington and Indianapolis: Indiana University Press, 1997.

Fields, Barbara Jeanne. "Slavery, Race, and Ideology in the United States of America." *New Left Review* 181 (May–June 1990): 95–118.

Fils-Aimé, Marc-Arthur, and Camille Chalmers. "Deklarasyon Pati Rasin Kan Pèp La Sou Konjonkti Politik Peyi A." *Rasanbleman Sosyalis pou yon Inisyativ Nasyonal tou Nèf*. Port-au-Prince, April 28, 2023.

Fisher, Sibylle. *Modernity Disavowed: Haiti and the Cultures of Slavery in the Age of Revolution*. Durham and London: Duke University Press, 2004.

Foote, Daniel, L. "Bodies Are Burned Alive in Haiti after the Biden Administration Did a Deal with the Devil . . . and I Should Know – I Was the US Special Envoy to the Troubled Country Until I Was Forced to Quit in Disgust." *Daily Mail*. April 28, 2023. https://dailymail.co.uk/news/article-12022367/As-bodies-burn-streets-Haiti-Biden-administration-blame-writes-former-diplomat.html.

Ford, Alessandro. "Kenya's Police Are No Match for Haiti's Urgan Nightmare." World Politics Review. August 11, 2023. https://www.worldpoliticsreview.com/haiti-gangs-crisis-corruption-violence-security-war/.

Fouchard, Jean. *Les Marrons du Syllabaire*. Port-au-Prince: Henri Deschamps, 1953.

France 24. "Calls for Haiti Intervention Mount, But No One Wants to Lead." July 26, 2023. https://www.france24.com/en/live-news/20230726-calls-for-haiti-intervention-mount-but-no-one-wants-to-lead.

Frank, Andre Gunder. *Capitalism and Underdevelopment in Latin America: Historical Studies of Chile and Brazil*. New York: Monthly Review Press, 1967.

Franklin, James. *The Present State of Hayti (Saint-Domingue), with Remarks on its Agriculture*. London: John Murray, 1828; rpt. Westport: Negro University Press/Greenwood Press, 1970.

Fraser, Nancy. "From Redistribution to Recognition? Dilemmas of Justice in a 'Postsocialist' Age." In *Justice Interruptus: Critical Reflections on the 'Postsocialist' Condition*. New York and London: Routledge, 1997.

———. "Rethinking Recognition." *New Left Review*, 3 (May–June 2000): 109.

———. "Against Progressive Neoliberalism, A New Progressive Populism." *Dissent*, January 8, 2017.

Friedman, Thomas L. "Foreign Affairs: Techno-Nothings." *The New York Times*, April 18, 1998, Section A, p. 13.

Gaillard, Roger. *Les Blancs débarquent, 7: 1919-1934: La Guérilla de Batraville*. Port-au-Prince: Imprimerie Le Natal, 1983.

Gaillard-Pourchet, Gusti-Klara. "'Dette de l'indépendance' d'Haïti (1825). Canonnière et huis clos pour une rançon coloniale." In *Haiti-France: Les chaînes de la dette. Le rapport Mackau (1825)*. Edited by Marcel Dorigny, Jean Marie Théodat, Gusti-klara Gaillard, and Jean Claude Buffaerts, 71–101. Paris: Maisonneuve & Larose, 2021.

Garcia, Marcus. "Le suspense reste entier: Qui à tué Jovenel Moïse?" *Haïti en Marche*, 22 Février 2023, XXXVII, No. 07.

———. "Penser Positif! Une certaine lecture derrière les sanctions Abinader!" *Haïti en Marche*. 26 Avril 2023. XXXVII, No. 16.

———. "Rodolphe Jaar prison à vie mais c'est le début d'un processus." *Haïti en Marche*, 14–20 Juin 2023, XXXVII, No. 23.

Gardella, Alexis. *Gender Assessment for USAID/Haiti Country Strategy Assessment*. Washington, DC: United States Agency for International Development, 2006.

Garrigus, John D. *Before Haiti: Race and Citizenship in French Saint-Domingue*. New York: Palgrave Macmillan, 2006.

Geggus, David Patrick. *Haitian Revolutionary Studies*. Bloomington and Indianapolis: Indiana University Press, 2002.

Genovese, Eugene D. *From Rebellion to Revolution: Afro-American Slave Revolts in the Making of the Modern World*. Baton Rouge: Louisiana State University Press, 1979.

Germain, Enomy. "Inflation, salaire minimum et sous-traitance en Haïti: la difficile èquation." *Le Nouvelliste* 4, no. 1 (2019).

Gilbert, Leah, Avid Reza, James Mercy, Veronica Lea, Juliette Lee, Likang Xu, Louis Herns Marcelin, Marissa Hast, John Vertefeuille, and Jean Wysler Domercant. "The Experience of Violence Against Children in Domestic Servitude in Haiti: Results from the Violence Against Children Survey, Haiti 2012." *Child Abuse and Neglect* 76 (2018): 184–185.

Gilroy, Paul. *The Black Atlantic: Modernity and Double Consciousness*. Cambridge: Harvard University Press, 1995.

Gimenez, Martha. "The Oppression of Women: A Structural Marxist View." In *Materialist Feminism: A Reader in Class, Difference, and Women's Lives*. Edited by Rosemary Hennessy and Chrys Ingraham. New York and London: Routledge, 1997.

Girault, Christian A. *Le commerce du café en Haïti: habitants, spéculateurs et exportateurs*. Paris: Editions de Centre National de la Recherche Scientifique, 1981.

Gisler, Antoine. *L'esclavage aux Antilles françaises, XVIIe-XIXe siècles*. Fribourg: Presses Universitaires Fribourg, 1965.

Goodhue, David, and Jacqueline Charles. "Coast Guard Stops Boat with 400 Haitians Off the Bahamas and Likely Headed to Florida." *Miami Herald*, January 23, 2023. https://www.miamiherald.com/news/nation-world/world/americas/haiti/article271514157.html.

Gramsci, Antonio. *Selections from the Prison Notebooks of Antonio Gramsci*. Edited and translated by Quintin Hoare and Geoffrey Nowell Smith. London and New York: Lawrence & Wishart, and International Publishers, 1971.

Habermas, Jürgen. *Theory and Practice*. Translated by John Vierted. Boston: Beacon Press, 1973.

Haiti. Embassy of the Republic of Haiti. https://www.haiti.org.

Haiti en Marche. "L'Entente du 9 Novembre à la merci des démolisseurs professionnels" and "Parti au pouvoir: Le PHTK est-il à vie?" 20 Novembre 2019, XXXIII, No. 45.

Hagelberg, G. B. "Sugar in the Caribbean: Turning Sunshine into Money." In *Caribbean Contours*. Edited by Sidney Mintz and Sally Price, 85–126. Baltimore: Johns Hopkins Univiversity Press, 1985.

Hall, Gwendolyn Midlo. *Social Control in Slave Plantation-Society: A Comparison of Saint-Domingue and Cuba*. Baltimore: Johns-Hopkins University Press, 1971.

Hall, Stuart. "Marx's Notes on Method: A 'Reading' of the '1857 Introduction,'" *Working Papers on Cultural Studies*, 6, 132–170.

———. *The Fateful Triangle: Race, Nation, Ethnicity.* Edited by Kobena Mercer. Cambridge: Harvard University Press, 2017.

Hannaford, Ivan. *Race: The History of an Idea in the West.* Washington, DC: The Woodrow Wilson Center Press, 1996.

Harris, H. S. "Hegel's System of Ethical Life: An Interpretation." In *System of Ethical Life (1802/3) and First Philosophy of Spirit (Part III of the System of Speculative Philosophy 1803/4).* Translated by H. S. Harris and T. M. Knox, 1–96. Albany: State University of New York, 1979.

Harvard Law School International Human Rights Clinic/Observatoire Haïtien des crimes contre l'humanité. *Killing with Impunity: State-Sanctioned Massacres in Haiti,* 2021. https://hrp.law.harvard.edu/wp-content/uploads/2022/10/Killing_With_Impunity-1.pdf.

Harvey, David. *Spaces of Global Capitalism: Towards a Theory of Uneven Geographical Development.* London: Verso, 2006.

———. *Seventeen Contradictions and the End of Capitalism.* Oxford and New York: Oxford University Press, 2014.

Hector, Michel. "Problème du passage à la société postesclavagiste et postcoloniale (1791-1793/1820-1826)." In *Genese de l'Etat haitien (1804-1859).* Edited by Michel Hector and Laennec Hurbon, 97–122. Port-au-Prince: Presses Nationales d'Haïti, 2009.

Hegel, G. W. F. *The Philosophy of History.* Translated by J. Sibree. New York: Dover Publications, Inc., 1956.

———. *The Phenomenology of Mind.* Translated by J. B. Baillie. New York: Harper & Row, Publishers, 1967.

———. *Lectures on the Philosophy of World History: Introduction: Reason in History.* Translated by H. B. Nisbet. Cambridge: Cambridge University Press, 1975.

———. *System of Ethical Life (1802/3) and First Philosophy of Spirit (Part III of the System of Speculative Philosophy 1803/4).* Translated by H. S. Harris and T. M. Knox, 1–96. Albany: State University of New York, 1979.

———. *Hegel: The Letters.* Translated by Clark Butler and Christiane Seiler, with commentary by Clark Butler. Bloomington: Indiana University Press, 1984.

———. *The Lectures on the Philosophy of Spirit 1827-28*. Translated and with an Introduction by Robert R. Williams. Oxford: Oxford University Press, 2007.

———. *Philosophy of Subjective Spirit, Volume 2: Anthropology*. Translated by M. J. Petry. Dordrecht: D. Reidel Publishing Co., 1978.

———. *The Philosophy of Right*. Translated with Notes by T. M. Knox. London, Oxford, New York: Oxford University Press, 1976.

Hilton, Rodney H. "Introduction to *The Transition from Feudalism*." London: New Left Books, 1976.

Honneth, Alex. *The Struggle for Recognition: The Moral Grammar of Social Conflicts*. Translated by Joel Anderson. Cambridge: Polity Press, 1995.

Hurbon, Laennec. "Les religions dans la construction de l'État (1801-1859)." In *Genèse de l'État haïtien (1804-1859)*. Edited by Michel Hector et Laënnec Hurbon, 189–202. Port-au-Prince: Presses Nationales d'Haiti.

Human Rights Watch. "Living a Nightmare: Haiti Needs an Urgent Rights-Based Response to Escalating Crisis." August 14, 2023. https://www.hrw.org/report/2023/08/14/living-nightmare/haiti-needs-urgent-rights-based-response-escalating-crisis.

Hume, David. *Esssays and Treaties on Several Subjects*. 2 vols. Dublin: J. Williams, 1742.

Inginac, Joseph-Baltazar. *Mémoires de Joseph Balzar Inginac*. Kingston: J. R. De Cordova, 1843.

Ioanes, Ellen. "Haiti's Gang Violence Crisis, Briefly Explained." Vox. March 26, 2023. https://www.vox.com/world-politics/2023/3/26/23657163/hsitis-gang-violence-crisis-explained.

Institute for Justice & Democracy in Haiti. "Human Rights and the Rule of Law in Haiti: Key Recent Developments December 2022 through May 2023." https://www.ijdh.org/wp-content/uploads/2020/02/Update-on-Human-Rights-and-Rule-of-Law-Situation_Feb-19-2020.pdf.

Inter-American Development Bank. *Country Strategy with Haiti, 2007-2011*. Washington, DC, 2007.

Isaac, Harold. "UN Chief Urges International Aid in Visit to Gang-Ravaged Haiti." *Reuters*, July 1, 2023. https://www.reuters.com/world/americas/un-chief-guterres-visits-gang-ravaged-haiti-2023-07-01/.

James, C. L. R. *The Black Jacobins: Toussaint Louverture and the San Domingo Revolution*. New York: Vintage Books, 1963.

Janetsky, Megan. "Gang War in Haitian Capital Leaves at Least 3 Police Dead." *San Diego Union-Tribune*, January 21, 2023. https://www.sandiegouniontribune.com/news/nation-world/story/2023-01-21/gang-war-in-haitian-capital-leaves-at-least-3-police-dead.

Janetsky, Megan, and Fernanda Pesce. "War for Control of Haiti's Capital Targets Women's Bodies." *AP News*, February 13, 2023. https://apnews.com/article/crime-violence-kidnapping-caribbean-haiti-89757f336975cb28283025e65446affb.

Jayaram, Kirsan C. "Fruits of Colonialism: The Production of Mangoes as Commodities in Northern Haiti." *Critique of Anthropology* 38, no. 4 (2018): 473–475.

Jean, Fritz. "L'Accord Montana n'autorise aucun adhérent à signer l'Accord du 21 décembre." *Haiti en Marche*, 4 Janvier 2023. No#52[62].pdf.

Jeanty, Gérard Junior. "Une nouvelle grille du salaire minimum entre en vigueur avec 500 gourdes pour les ouvriers de la sous-traitance." *Le Nouvelliste*, 6 Novembre 2019.

Jefferson, Thomas. "Notes on the State of Virginia." In *Writings*, 123–325. New York: Library Classics of the United States, Inc., 1984.

Joachim, Benoît. "L'indemnité de Saint-Domingue et la question des rapatriés." *Revue Historique*, 246 (Octobre-Décembre 1971): 359–376.

———. *Les racines du sous-développement en Haiti*. Port-au-Prince: Imprimerie H. Deschamps, 1979.

Johnston, Jake, and Chris François. "Haiti News Round-up: Two Years Since the Assassination of Haiti's President." Center for Economic and Policy Research. July 18, 2023. http://cepr.net/haiti-news-round-up-two-years-since-the-assassination-of-haitis-president/?emci=9b34b8ae-ee11-a9bb-00224832eb73&emdi=e24b8063-9725-ee11-a9bb-00224832eb73&ceid=4627713.

——. "Haiti News Roundup: Thousands Displaced due to Violence." Center for Economic and Policy Research. August 18, 2023. https://cepr.net/haiti-news-roundup-thousands-displaced-due-to-violence/.

Kant, Immanuel. *Essays and Treatises on Moral, Political, Religious, and Various Philosophical Subjects*. Vol. 2. London: William Richardson, 1799.

Katz, Jonathan M. "With Cheap Food Imports, Haiti Can't Feed Itself." *The Associated Press*, March 20, 2010.

——. "Humanitarian Malfeasance: The United Nations Is Responsible for Killing More Than 8,000 Haitians Since 2010. And It's Not Even Willing to Say It's Sorry." Slate.com, February 23, 2013. https://nam02.safelinks.protection.outlook.com/?url=https%3A%2F%2Fslate.com.news-and-politics%2F2013%2F02%2Fban-ki-moon-rejects-haitian-cholera-claims-the-united-nations-brought-a-dealy-strain-of-cholera-to-haiti-that-killed-8000-people-but-accepts-no-responsibility-for-the-disaster.html&data=05%7C01%7Cmmenzel%40rowman.com%7Cbc38 1f38912447e8662108dbf2b38885%7C8fdc2247c6bb43e686abb8ce3c37e4bf%7C 0%7C0%7C638370625150324612%7CUnknown%7CTWFpbGZsb3d8eyJWIjo iMC4wLjAwMDAiLCJQIjoiV2luMzIiLCJBTiI6Ik1haWwiLCJXVCI6Mn0%3D %7C3000%7C%7C%7C&sdata=H07kbpQ23F0n%2FYINhG4AAk9ICkcuoV9%2B Cjjj7EbQtUY%3D&reserved=0.

——. "Haiti's Elites Keep Calling for the U.S. Marines." *Foreign Policy*, October 31, 2022. https://foreignpolicy.com/2022/10/31/haiti-us-intervention-gangs-united-nations/.

Knight, Franklin. *The Caribbean: The Genesis of a Fragmented Nationalism*. Oxford and New York: Oxford University Press, 1978.

Kojeve, Alexandre. *Introduction to the Reading of Hegel: Lectures on the Phenomenology of Spirit*. Translated by James H. Nichols Jr. New York and London: Basic Books, 1969.

Kurmanaev, Anatoly. "Haitian Prime Minister Had Close Links With Murder Suspect." *The New York Times*, January 10, 2022. https://www.nytimes.com/2022/01/10/world/americas/haitian-prime-minister-assassination-suspect.html.

Labelle, Micheline. *Idéologie de couleur et classes sociales en Haïti*. Montréal: Les Presses de l'Université de Montréal, 1978.

Lacroix, François-Joseph Pamphile, baron de. *Mémoires pour servir à l'histoire de la révolution de Saint-Domingue*. 2 vols. Paris: Pillet Aîné, 1820.

LaFeber, Walter. *Inevitable Revolutions: The United States in Central America.* New York: W. W. Norton and Co., 1984.

Las Casas, Bartolome de. *The Devastation of the Indies: A Brief Account.* Translated by Herma Briffault. New York: Seabury Press, 1974.

Latin American Advisor. "Could a Kenya-Led Force Increase Security in Haiti?" August 17, 2023. https://thedialogue.org/wp-content/uploads/2023/08/LAA230817.pdf.

Laurent, Gérard M. *Six études sur Jean-Jacques Dessalines.* Port-au-Prince: Imprimerie Les Presses Libres, n.d.

Lederer, Edith. "Canada, U.S. Show No Interest in Leading Haiti Security Force at UN Security Council." Global News. January 24, 2023. https://globalnews.ca/news/9434251/haiti-crisis-canada-us-united-nations/.

Lee, Heidi. "Canada Sends Long-Range Patrol Aircraft to Support Haiti as Gang Violence Escalates." Global News. February 5, 2023. https://globalnews.ca/news/9462105/canada-partol-aircraft-haiti-violence/.

Léger, Abel-Nicolas. *Histoire Diplomatique d'Haïti.* Tome premier (1804-1859). Port-au-Prince: Imprimerie A. Héraux, 1930.

Léger, J. N. *Haïti, son histoire et ses détracteurs.* New York: Neale Publishing Co., 1907).

Le Monde. "En Haïti, au moins 42 personnes sont mortes depuis la nouvelle vague de contestation mi-septembre." 1 novembre 2019. https://www.lemonde.fr/international/article/2019/11/01/en-haiti-au-moins-42-personnes-sont-mortes-depuis-la-nouvelle-vague-de-contestation-mi-septembre_6017757_3210.html.

Le Noir de Rouvray, Laurent-François. *Une correspondance familiale au temps des troubles de Saint-Domingue: Lettres du Marquis et de la Marquise de Rouvray à leur fille, Saint-Domingue-Etats-Unis, 1791-1796.* Edited by M. E. McIntosh and B.C. Weber. Paris: Société de l'Histoire des Colonies Françaises et Librairie Larose, 1959.

Le Nouveliste. "Plusieurs members de gangs abbatus par la police, d'autres appréhendés." 4 Janvier 2023. lenouvelliste.com.

———. "82,4% des Haïtiens veulent quitter le pays." 27 Janvier 2021.

Léon, Pierre. *Marchands et spéculateurs dauphinoise dans le monde antillais du XIIIe siècle*. Paris, 1963.

Léopold-Hector, Marion. "La résistance paysanne en Haïti: éléments pour une analyse." Série G. Working Papers no. 9, University of Ottawa: Institute for International Co-operation, March 1977.

Lewis, Gordon K. *Main Currents in Caribbean Thought: The Historical Evolution of Caribbean Society in its Ideological Aspects, 1492-1900*. Baltimore: Johns Hopkins University Press, 1983.

Leyburn, James G. *The Haitian People*. New Haven: Yale University Press, 1941.

Liedman, Sven-Eric. *A World to Win: The Life and Works of Karl Marx*. London: Verso, 2018.

Louis, Chadrac. "Les paysans de l'Artibonite subissent les consequences du banditisme." *Le Nouvelliste*, 24 février 2023.

Luc, Jean. *Structure économique et lutte nationale populaire en Haïti*. Montréal: Les Éditions Nouvelle Optique, 1976.

Lundahl, Matts. *Peasants and Poverty: A Study of Haiti*. New York: St. Martin's Press, 1979.

———. *The Haitian Economy: Man, Land and Markets*. New York: St. Martin's Press, 1983.

Luscombe, Richard. "Mastermind of Assassination of Haiti President Sentenced to Life by US Court." *The Guardian*, June 2, 2023. https://www.theguardian.com/worl/2023/jun/02/haiti-president-assassination-rodolphe-jaar-life-sentence.

Luxemburg, Rosa. "Women's Suffrage and Class Struggle." In *Selected Political Writings of Rosa Luxemburg*. Edited by Dick Howard. New York: Monthly Review Press, 1971.

Madiou, Thomas. *Histoire d'Haïti*, 8 vols. Port-au-Prince: Editions Henri Deschamps, 1988.

Malie, Kenan. *The Meaning of Race: Race, History and Culture in Western Society*. New York: New York University Press, 1996.

Manigat, Leslie. *La politique agraire du gouvernement d'Alexandre Pétion*. Port-au-Prince: Imprimerie La Phalange, 1962.

Marcus. "La crise politique haïtienne débarque á Washington, DC" *Haiti en Marche*, 30 Octobre-5 Novembre 2019, XXXIII, No. 42.

Marcuse, Herbert. *Reason and Revolution: Hegel and the Rise of Social Theory*. New York: Oxford University Press, 1941/Beacon Press, 1961.

Marius, Philippe-Richard. *The Unexceptional Case of Haiti: Race and Class Privilege in Postcolonial Bourgeois Society*. Jackson: University of Mississippi Press, 2022.

Mars, Louis-Henri. "To Curb Gang Violence in Haiti, Break with Politics as Usual." *Just Security*, April 16, 2023. https://www.justsecurity.org/86017/to-curb-gang-violence-in-haiti-break-with-politics-as-usual/.

Martinez, Samuel. *Peripheral Migrants: Haitians and Dominican Republic Sugar Plantations*. Knoxville: University of Tennessee Press, 1995.

Marx, Karl. *Grundrisse: Foundations of the Critique of Political Economy*. Translated by Martin Nicolaus. Harmondsworth: Penguin Books, 1973.

———. "Economic and Philosophic Manuscripts of 1844." In Karl Marx and Frederick Engels, *Collected Works, V. 3: Marx and Engels: 1843-44,* 229–346. New York: International Publishers, 1975.

———. *Capital: A Critique of Political Economy, Volume One*. Introduction by Ernest Mandel. Translated by Ben Fowkes. London: Penguin Books, 1976.

———. "Critique of the Gotha Programme." In *Karl Marx: Selected Writings*. Edited by David McLellan, 564–570. Oxford and New York: Oxford University Press, 1977.

Mathon, Alix. *Haïti, un cas*. Port-au-Prince: Imprimerie Le Natal, 1985.

Mbeki, Thabo. "Address by the President of South Africa, Thabo Mbeki, at the Celebrations of the Bicentenary of the Independence of Haiti." Port-au-Prince, Haiti, January 1, 2004.

Mbembe, Arhille. *Critique of Black Reason*. Translated by Laurent Dubois. Durham: Duke University Press, 2017.

McGuigan, Claire. *Agricultural Liberalisation in Haiti*. London: Christian Aid, 2006.

Mélodie 103.3 FM, "Edmond Mulet annonce une nouvelle Occupation militaire américaine!," 17 Décembre 2019, XXXIII, No. 48, p. 6.

———. "Une occupation militaire américaine et rien d'autre, insiste Mulet parce que, dit-il, la seule à avoir la capacité logistique pour la tâche à accomplir. A bon entendeur!" Ibid.

———."Comprendre le débat sur le salaire minimum des ouvriers." Haiti en Marche 2022. Vol XXXVI, 2 Mars 2022. HEM No. 08_2022_03_02.pdf.

———. "Les services du FMI parviennent à un accord avec Haïti Pout un nouveau programme sous contrôle." 12 Juillet 2023. HEM 27_2023_07_12.pdf.

Mérancourt, Widlore, and Amanda Coletta. "Haitians Fight Back Against Gangs, Drawing Support—and Worry." *The Washington Post*, May 18, 2023. https://www.washingtonpost.com/world/2023/05/15/haiti-vigilantes-gangs-mob-lynching/.

Métral, Antoine. *Histoire de l'Insurrection des esclaves dans le Nord de Saint-Domingue*. Paris: F. Scherff, 1818.

Michel, Andrée. "Introduction." *Nouvelle Questions Féministes*, 11/12: La Militarisation et les Violences à l'égard des Femmes. *Hivers*, 1985, 4–8.

Midy, Franklin. "Marrons de la liberté, révoltés de la liberation: Le Marron inconnu revisité." In *Genèse de l'État haïtien (1804-1859)*. Edited by Michel Hector and Laennec Hurbon, 123–148. Port-au-Prince: Éditions Presses Nationales d'Haiti, 2009.

Millet, Kathy. *Les paisans haïtiens et l'occupation américaine, 1915–1930*. Québec: Collectif Paroles, 1978.

Mintz, Sidney W. *Caribbean Transformations*. Chicago: Aldine Publishing Co., 1974.

———. "The So-Called World System: Local Initiative and Local Response." *Dialectical Anthropology* 4 (November 1977): 253–270.

———. "Was the Plantation Slave a Proletarian?" *Review* 2 (Summer 1978): 81–98.

———. *Sweetness and Power: The Place of Sugar in Modern History*. New York: Viking Press, 1985.

Moïse, Claude. *Constitutions et luttes de pouvoir en Hait (1804-1915), Tome I: La Faillite des Classes Dirigeantes*. Montréal: Les éditions du CIDIHCA, 1988.

———. "Titre III Du Citoyen—Des Droits et Devoirs Fondamentaux, Chapitre I: De la Qualité de Citoyen, Arts, 1 et X, Constitution de la Républake d'Haïti 1987, in Claude Moïse, *Constitution et Luttes de pouvoir en Haïti, Tome 2 1915-1987: de *l'Occupation Étrangère à la Dictature Macoute*. Montréal: Le Centre International de Documentation et d'Information Haïtienne, Caraïbéenne et Afro-Canadienne, 1990.

Moïse, Claude, and Emile Olivier. *Repenser Haïti: Grandeur et misères d'un mouvement démocratique*. Montréal: Les Éditions du CIDHICA, 1992.

Montague, Ludwell Lee. *Haiti and the United States 1714-1938*. Durham: Duke University Press, 1940.

Montesquieu, Charles de Secondat, Baron de. *De l'Esprit des lois*. 2 vols. Introduction by Robert Derathé. Paris: Éditions Garnier Frères, 1973.

Moore, Barrington Jr. *Social Origins of Dictatorship and Democrac: Lord and Peasants in the Making of the Modern World*. Boston: Beacon Press, 1966.

Moore, O. Ernest. *Haiti: Its Stagnant Society and Shackled Economy*. New York: Exposition Press, 1972.

Moral, Paul. *Le paysan haïtien: étude sur la vie rurale en Haïti*. Paris: G. P. Maisonneuve et Larose, 1961.

Moreau de Saint-Méry, Médéric-Louis-Elie. *Description topographique, physique, civile, politique et historique de la partie française de l'Île de Saint-Domingue*. 3 vols. Paris: Dupont, 1797. Rpt. Société de l'Histoire des Colonies Françaises et Librairie Larose, 1958.

Moreno Fraginals, Manuel. *The Sugar Mill: The Socio-economic Complex in Cuba*. Translated by Cedric Belfrage. New York: Monthly Review Press, 1976.

———. "Plantations in the Caribbean: Cuba, Puerto-Rico, and the Dominican Republic in the Late Nineteenth Century." In *Betweeen Slavery and Free Labor: The Spanish-Speaking Caribbean in the Nineteenth Century*. Edited by Manuel Moreno Fraginals, Frank Moya Pons, and Stanley L. Engerman, 3–21. Baltimore: Johns Hopkins University Press, 1985.

Morland, Sarah, and Harold Isaac. "Haiti's Deadly Vigilante Movement Sees Decline in Gang Violence, Report Says." *Reuters*, May 28, 2023. https://www.reuters.com/world/americas/haitis-deadly-vigilante-movement-sees-decline-gang-violence-report-2023-05-28/.

Mousnier, Roland. *Histoire générale des civilisations, vol. 4: Les XVIe et XVIIe siècles*. Paris: Presses Universitaires de France, 1965.

Moya Pons, Frank. "Deuda Pública, Crisis Económica y Oposición durante la Dominación Haitiana." *Renovación* 198 (4 de Mayo de 1972): 28–32.

———. *The Dominican Republic: A National History*. Princeton: Marcus Wiener Publishers, 1998.

Muggah, Robert. "Haiti Is on the Brink of State Failure." *Foreign Policy*, February 12, 2023. https://foreignpolicy.com/2023/02/17/haiti-crisis-corruption-criminal-gangs-violence-humanitarian-assistance-state-failure-sanctions/.

Nation Africa, "Kenya court temporarily blocks police deployment to Haiti." *The East African*, October 9, 2023. https://www.theeastafrican.co.ke/tea/news/east-africa/kenya-court-temporarily-blocks-police-deployment-to-haiti-4396294.

Nau, Emile. *Histoire des Caciques d'Haïti*. Paris: Gustave Guerin et Cie, 1894.

Nesbitt, Nick. "Troping Toussaint, Reading Revolution." *Research in African Literature* 35, no. 2 (Summer 2004): 18–33.

New York Carib News. "Haiti—Toll Stations on Main Roads Imposed by Gangs." February 25, 2023. nycaribenews.com/2023/02/haiti-toll-stations-on-main-roads-imposed-by-gangs/.

Nicholls, David. *From Dessalines to Duvalier: Race, Colour and National Independence in Haiti*. New York and London: Cambridge University Press, 1979.

O'Connor, Maura R. "Subsidizing Starvation: How American Tax Dollars Are Keeping Arkansas Rice Growers Fat and Starving Millions of Haitians." *Foreign Policy*, June 9, 2013.

Okin, Susan Moller. "Political Liberalism, Justice, Gender." *Ethics* 105 (October 1994): 42.

Outlaw, Lucius. "African Philosophy: Deconstructive and Reconstructive Challenges." In *Sage Philosophy: Indigenous Thinkers and Modern Debate on African Philosophy*. Edited by H. Odera Oruka, 223–248. Leiden and New York: E.J. Brill, 1990.

Parkin, Frank. *Marxism and Class Theory: A Bourgeois Critique*. New York: Columbia University Press, 1979.

Parry, J. H. "Transport and Trade Routes." In *The Cambridge Economic History of Europe, Vol. 4: The Economy of Expanding Europe in the Sixteenth and

Seventeenth Centuries. Edited by E. E. Rich and C. H. Wilson, 155–219. Cambridge: Cambridge University Press, 1967.

Patterson, Orlando. *Slavery and Social Death: A Comparative Study*. Cambridge: Harvard University Press, 1982.

PBS News Hour. PBS News Hour, "Why Haitians say they won't stop protesting," December 5, 2019, https://www.pbs.org/newshour/world/why-haitians-say-they-wont-stop-protesting.

Péan, Leslie. *Haïti:* Économie *politique de la corruption: De Saint-Domingue à Haïti, 1791-1870*. Paris: Maisonneuve et Larose, 2000.

———. *Haïti:* Économie *politique de la corruption: L'État marron (1870-1915)*. Tome II. Paris: Maisonneuve et Larose, 2005.

———. *Haïti:* Économie *politique de la corruption: Le saccage*. Tome III. Paris: Maisonneuve et Larose, 2006.

———. *Haïti:* Économie *politique de la corruption: L'ensauvagement macoute et ses conséquences—1957-1990*. Tome IV. Paris: Maisonneuve et Larose, 2007.

Peltz, Jennifer. "Haiti's Leader: Migration Won't End Unless Inequality Does." *AP News*, September 25, 2021. https://apnews.com/article/immigration-united-nations-general-assembly-poverty-united-nations-haiti-67d1408dd473832a474652197ba180bd.

Phillips, Anthony D. "Haiti's Independene Debt and Prospects for Restitution." Institute for Justice & Democracy in Haiti. May 2009. Accessed May 11, 2018.

Pierre, Alfred. "Les non-dits de la question de salaire minimum: carte blanche à l'émigration irrégulière?" *Le Nouvelliste*, 22 Août 2017. Lenouvelliste.com.

Pierre, Guy. *Histoire de l'industrie minière en Haïti: Accumulation éclaire du capital et frustration économique (1956-1982)*. Montréal: Les Éditions du CIDIHCA, 2017.

Pierre-Charles, Gérard. "Genèse des nations haïtienne et dominicaine." *Nouvelle Optique* 8 (Octobre-Novembre, 1972).

———. *L'économie d'Haïti et sa voie de dévelppement*. Paris: Maisonneuve et Larose, 1967.

Piketty, Thomas. *Capital and Ideology*. Translated by Arthur Goldhammer. Cambridge, MA: Belknap Press of Harvard University Press, 2020.

Pinkard, Terry. *Hegel: A Biography*. Cambridge: Cambridge University Press, 2000.

Placide, Justin. *Histoire politique et statistique de l'Ile d'Haïti, Saint-Domingue, écrite sur les documents officiels et des notes communiquées pa sir James Barskett*. Paris: Brière, 1826.

Pluchon, Pierre. *Toussaint Louverture: de l'esclavage au pouvoir*. Paris: Éditions de l'École, 1979.

Plummer, Brenda Gayle. *Haiti and the Great Powers, 1902-1915*. Baton Rouge: Louisiana State University Press, 1988.

Pomeranz, Kenneth. *The Great Divergence: China, Europe, and the Making of the Modern World Economy*. Princeton: Princeton University Press, 2000.

Porter, Catherine, Constant Méheut, Matt Apuzzo, and Selam Gebrekidan. "The Ransom: The Roots of Haiti's Misery: Reparations to Enslavers." *The New York Times*, May 20, 2022. https://www.nytimes.com/2022/05/20/world/americas/haiti-history-colonized-france.html.

Portes, Alejandro, and John Walton. *Labor, Class, and the International System*. New York: Academic Press, Inc., 1981.

Price-Mars, Jean. *La République d'Haïti et la République Dominicaine*. Tome 1. Port-au-Prince: Les Éditions Fardin, 2009.

Radio Métropole. "Réparations pour la dette de l'indépendance: le gouvernement français répond à M. Aristide." Port-au-Prince, Haiti, 9 avril 2003.

Ramsey, Kate. *The Spirits and the Law: Vodou and Power in Haiti*. Chicago: University of Chicago Press, 2011.

Rauch, Leo. "Introduction: On Hegel's Concept of Spirit." In Leo Rauch, *Hegel and the Human Spirit: A Translation of the Jena Lectures on the Philosophy of Spirit (1805-6)*, 15–81. Detroit: Wayne State University Press, 1983.

Regan, Jane. "Shooting at Haitian Parliament Surprises Few as Anti-Government Protests Continue." NACLA, September 26, 2019. https://nacla.org/news/2019/09/26/shooting-haitian-parliament-surprises-few-anti-government-protests-continue.

Reliefweb. "Statement on Multi-National Force to Support Haiti, 04 August 2023." August 5, 2023. www.reliefweb.int/report/haiti/statement-multi-national-force-support-haiti-04-august-2023.

Repussard, Faustin. "Lettre au Général de Division Rochambeau, 6 juin 1802." *Rochambeau Papers*. University of Florida, Gainsville.

Rivers, Matt, Etant Dupain, and Natalie Gallón. "Haitian Prime Minister Involved in Planning the President's Assassination Says Judge Who Oversaw Case." *CNN*, February 8, 2022. https://www.cnn.com/2022/02/08/americas/haiti-assassination-investigation-prime-minister-intl-cmd-latam/index.html.

Robles, Frances, and André Paultre. "Vigilante Justice Rises in Haiti and Crime Plummets." *The New York Times*, June 3, 2023. https://www.nytimes.com/2023/06/03/world/americas/haiti-crime-gangs-vigilantes.html.

Robertson, Dylan. "Canada Delivers More Armoured Vehicles to Haiti as Police Try to Push Back Gangs." *Moosejaw Today*, January 12, 2023. https://moosejawtoday.com/national-news/canada-delivers-more-armoured-vehicles-to-haiti-as-police-try-to-push-back-gangs-6364391.

———. "Haiti at Risk of Famine as Farmers Kidnapped, 'Extremely Bad' Hunger Fuels Tumult." *National Post*, May 13, 2023. https://nationalpost.com/news/world/haiti-at-risk-of-famine-as-farmers-kidnapped-extremely-bad-hunger-fuels-tumult.

Robinson, Randall. "Honor Haiti, Honor Ourselves, Forget Haiti, Forget Ourselves." *Counter Punch*, January 1, 2004.

Roediger, David. *The Wages of Whiteness: Race and the Making of the American Working Class*. London and New York: Verso, 1991.

Roth, Richard, and Hira Humayun. "Haiti's Crime Rate More than Doubles in a Year." *CNN*, April 26, 2023. https://cnn.com/2023/04/26/world/haiti-crime-rate-doubles-intl/index.html.

Rueschemeyer, Dietrich, Evelyn Huber Stephens, and John. D. Stephens. *Capitalist Development and Democracy*. Chicago: University of Chicago Press, 1992.

Saint-Louis, Vertus. *Mer et liberté en Haïti (1492-1794)*. Port-au-Prince, 2008.

Saint-Rémy, Joseph. *Pétion et Haïti: Études monographique et historique*. 15 vols. 2nd ed. Paris: Librairie Berger-Levrault, 1956.

Sala-Molin, Louis. *Le Code Noir ou le calvaire de Cannan*. Paris: Presses Universitaires de France, 1987.

Sanon, Evans. "Neighborhood Fights Gangs after Vigilante Killings." *Chattanoga Times Free Press*, April 27, 2023. https://www.timesfreepress.com/news/2023/apr/27/neighborhood-fights-haiti-gangs-tfp/.

Sannon, H. Pauleus. *Histoire de Toussaint-Louverture*. 3 vols. Port-au-Prince: Imprimerie A. Héraux, 1933.

Sauer, Carl Ortwin. *The Spanish Main*. Berkeley: University of California Press, 1969.

Schneider, Mark L. "Haitians Are Central to Ending Their Country's Crisis, But They Cannot Do It Alone." *Miami Herald*, August 2, 2023. https://miamiherald.com/opinion/op-ed/article277857333.html.

Schoelcher, Victor. *Vie de Toussaint Louverture*. 2nd ed. Paris: Paul Ollendorff, 1889.

———. *Colonies Étrangères et Haïti, Résultats de l'émancipation anglaise*. Paris: Pagnerre, Éditeur, 1843.

Scott, Helen. "Haiti Under Siege." *International Socialist Review* 35 (May-June 2004): 3. https://isreview.org/issues/35/haiti_under_siege/.

Scott, Rebecca J. "Explaining Abolition: Contradictions, Adaptation, and Challenge in Cuban Slave Society, 1860-1886." In *Between Slavery and Free Labor: The Spanish-Speaking Caribbean in the Nineteenth Century*. Edited by Manuel Moreno Fraginals, Frank Moya Pons, and Stanley L. Engerman, 25–53. Baltimore: Johns Hopkins University Press, 1985.

Shoaff, Jennifer. "In the Face of a Haitian Child: Racial Intimacies, Paternalistic Intervention, and Discourse of 'Deviant Black Motherhood' in Transnational Hispaniola." *Feminist Studies* 43, no. 2 (2017): 159–172.

Shuldiner, Henry "UN-Backed Haiti Force Unlikely to Root Out Gangs." *InSight Crime*, October 4, 2023. https://www.insightcrime.org/news/un-backed-haiti-force-unlikely-to-root-out-gangs/.

Singh, Raju Jan, and Mary Barton-Dock. *Haiti: Toward a New Narrative*. Washington, DC, International Bank for Reconstruction and Development/The World Bank, 2015.

Smith, Adam. *An Inquiry into the Nature and Causes of the Wealth of Nations: A Selected Edition*. Oxford and New York: Oxford University Press, 1998.

Smith, Marie-Danielle. "Trudeau to Deploy Navy Vessels to Haiti for Intelligence Gathering." *CTV News*, February 16, 2023. https://www.ctvnews.ca/politics/trudeau-to-deploy-navy-vessels-to-haiti-for-intelligence-gathering-1.6276246.

Soboul, Alfred. *The French Revolution 1789-1799: From the Storming of the Bastille to Napoleon*. Translated by Alan Forrest and Colin Jones. London: Unwin Hyman, 1989.

Steckley, Marylynn, and Yasmine Shamsie. "Manufacturing Corporate Landscapes: The Case of Agrarian Displacement and Food (In)Security in Haiti." *Third World Quarterly* 36, no. 1 (2015).

Tavares, Pierre Franklin. "Hegel et Haiti ou le silence de Hegel sur Saint-Domingue." *Chemins Critiques* 2, no. 3 (Mai 1992): 113–131.

Taylor, Luke. "Kenya's Offer to Send Police to Haiti Sparks Human Rights Concerns." *The Guardian*, August 5, 2023. http://www.theguardian.com/world/2023/aug/05/kenya-police-haiti-human-rights-concerns.

The Associated Press. "Canada Military Plane Returns after Haiti Surveillance." *Seattle Times*, February 7, 2023. https://www.seattletimes.com/nation-world/canada-military-plane-returns-after-haiti-surveillance/.

Thomas, Clive Y. *Power and the Powerless: Economic Policy and Change in the Caribbean*. New York: Monthly Review Press, 1988.

Thomas, Gessika, and Brian Ellsworth. "Haiti's Henry Urges Elections amid Calls for Transition Government." *Reuters*, February 7, 2022. https://www.reuters.com/world/americas/haitis-henry-urges-elections-amid-calls-transition-government-2022-02-07/.

Thompson, Alvin. "The Berbice Revolt, 1763-64." *Themes in African-Guyanese History* (1998): 77–105.

Thornton, John. *Africa and Africans in the Making of the Atlantic World, 1400-1800*. Cambridge: Cambridge University Press, 1998.

Tibebu, Teshale. *Hegel and the Third World: The Making of Eurocentrism in World History*. Syracuse: Syracuse University Press, 2011.

Tomich, Dale W. *Through the Prism of Slavery: Labor, Capital, and World Economy*. Lanham, MD: Rowman & Littlefield Publishers, Inc., 2004.

———. "Thinking the 'Unthinkable': Victor Schoelcher and Haiti." *Review: Fernand Braudel Center for the Study of Economies, Historical Systems, and Civilizations* 31, no. 3 (2008): 401–431.

Toussaint, Eddy (Tontongi). "La France doit restituer à Haïti la rançon de l'indemnité." *AlterPresse*, 30 août 2010.

Trouillot, Michel-Rolph. *Les Racines Historiques de l'État Duvalierien*. Port-au-Prince: Henri Deschamps, 1986.

———. *Haiti: State Against Nation: The Origins and Legacy of Duvalierism*. New York: Monthly Review Press, 1990.

———. *Ti Difé Boulé sou istoua ayiti*. New York: Koleksion Lakansiel, 1977.

———. "From Planters' Journals to Academia: The Haitian Revolution as Unthinkable History." *Journal of Caribbean History* 25 (1991): 81–99.

———. *Silencing the Past: Power and the Production of History*. Boston: Beacon Press, 1995.

Turnier, Alain. *La Société des Baillonnettes*. Port-au-Prince: Imprimerie Le Natal, 1985.

UN Humanitarian. "'This Is Not a Country Where You Can Dream': The Shattered Hopes of the Haitian People," April 7, 2023. https://unocha.exposure.co/this-is-not-a-country-where-you-can-dream.

UN News Global. "Pledging Conference for Haiti Reconstruction." February 16, 2022. https://news.un.org/en/story/2022/02/1112062.

———. "UN Calls for Support for International Force for Haiti." December 21, 2022. https://news.un.org/en/story/2022/12/1131922.

UNICEF. "Kidnappings of Children and Women Spiking at Alarming Rates in Haiti." August 7, 2023. https://www.unicef.org.uk/press-releases/kidnappings-of-children-and-women-spiking-at-alarming-rates-in-haiti-unicef/.

Vant Bèf Info. "Installation imminente du Haut Conseil de Transition." *Haïti en Marche*, 29 décembre 2022. https://vantbefinfo.com/haiti-politique-installation-imminente-du-haut-conseil-de-transition/.

Vendryes, B. *De L'Indemnité de Saint-Domingue*. Paris: Chez l'Auteur, 1839.

Vincent, Stenio. "Statement of Mr. Stenio Vincent, New York, N.Y., Representing the Union Patriotique d'Haiti, Former Minister of Justice and Interior, Minister to the Hague, and President of the Senate, Republic of Haiti." *Inquiry Into the Occupation of Haiti and Santo Domingo*. Hearing Before a Select Committee on Haiti and Santo Domingo, United States Senate. Sixty-Seventh Congress, First Session Pursuant to S. RES. 112 Authorizing a Special Committee to Inquire Into the Occupation and Administration of the Republic of Haiti and the Dominican Republic, Part I, August 5, 1921. Washington, DC, Government Printing Office, 1921.

Voltaire, François-Marie Arouet. *Essai sur les mœurs et l'esprit des nations*. Edited with an Introduction and Notes by René Pomeau. Paris: Éditions Garnier Frères, 1963.

Voss, Gavin. "Haiti's Rural Gangs Threaten Food Production as Hunger Crisis Looms." *St Kitts & Nevis Observer*, February 28, 2023.

Wallerstein, Immanuel. *The Modern World-System, I: Capitalist Agriculture and the Origins of the European World-Economy*. New York: Academic Press, 1974.

———. "The Rise and Future Demise of the World-Capitalist System: Concepts for Comparative Analysis." In *The Capitalist World-Economy: Essays by Immanuel Wallerstein*, 1–36. Cambridge University Press, 1976.

———. *The Decline of America Power: The U.S. in a Changing World*. New York and London: New Press, 2003.

Wallez, Jean-Baptiste Guislain. *Précis Historique des Négociations entre la France et Saint-Domingue*. Paris: Ponthieu, 1826.

Waters, Mary. *Ethnic Options: Choosing Identities in America*. Berkeley: University of California Press, 1990.

Weber, Max. *From Max Weber: Essays in Sociology*. Translated and edited by H. H. Gerth and C. Wright Mills. New York: Oxford University Press, 1946.

Williams, Eric. *Capitalism and Slavery*. New York: Capricorn Books, 1966.

———. *From Columbus to Castro: The History of the Caribbean 1492-1969*. New York: Harper & Row, Publishers, 1970.

Wood, Ellen Meiksins. *Democracy against Capitalism*. Cambridge: Cambridge University Press, 1995.

———. *The Origin of Capitalism: A Longer View*. London: Verso, 2002.

———. *Empire of Capital*. London: Verso, 2003.

———. *Liberty and Property: A Social History of Western Political Thought from Renaissance to Enlightenment*. London: Verso, 2012.

World Bank. *Haiti: Agriculture and Rural Development: Diagnostic and Proposals for Agricultural and Rural Development Policies and Strategies*. Washington, DC: World Bank, 2005.

———. *Investing in People to Fight Poverty in Haiti: Reflections for Evidence-Based Policy Making*. Washington, DC: World Bank, 2014.

World Bank Group. *Agricultural Financing in Haiti: Diagnosis and Recommendation*. Washington, DC, 2019.

World Food Program. *Haiti on the Brink: Hunger Levels Rising, Warns Report*, March 23, 2023. https://www.wfp.org/news/haiti-brink-hunger-levels-rising-warns-report.

Wucker, Michele. *Why the Cocks Fight: Dominicans, Haitians, and the Struggle for Hispaniola*. New York: Hill and Wang, 1999.

Yates, Caitlyn. "Haitian Migration through the Americas: A Decade in the Making." Migration Policy Institute. September 30, 2021. https://www.migrationpolicy.org/article/haitian-migration-through-americas.

Index

Accord, Montana, 86
Acte de Déchéance. See Bill of Impeachment
ADIH. *See* Association of Haitian Industries
Agency for International Development (USAID), U.S., 106
agricultural sector, tariffs lowered in, 56, 107
Alphonse, Roberson, 95
androcentric norms, women devalued by, 70–71
Anglade, Mireille Neptune, 2–3, 61, 63–64
Ardouin, Beaubrun, 7, 25–26, 27
Aristide, Jean-Bertrand, 43, 54, 57, 85, 97–98; indemnity rejected by, 8; Marines accompanying, 44, 55–56; neoliberal policies caved to by, 2; restitution demanded by, 8–9, 38, 40n12
assembly industry, in Haiti, 54, 81–83, 106, 108

Assembly of the People's Socialist Party for a New National Initiative (*Rasanbleman Sosyalis pou yon Inisyativ Nasyonal tou Nèf*), 96–97
Association of Haitian Industries (*Association des Industries d'Haïti*) (ADIH), 82, 108–9
Attis, Evelyne, 83
Auguste, Claude, 13
Auguste, Marcel, 13
L'autre moitié du développement (Anglade), 2, 61

Bahamas, 100
Bald-Head Haitian Party (*Fanmi Lavalas*), 98, 111n2
Banque Nationale, 46
Barros, Jacques, 30
"basic needs" model, 54
Baudin, Charles, 22, 24
de Beauvoir, Simone, 62
Beauvois, Frédérique, 30
Bell, Beverly, 72, 83, 85–86

151

Bellerive, Jean-Max, 58
Biden, Joseph, 92, 99–100
Bill of Impeachment (*Acte de Déchéance*), 31
Bonaparte, Napoleon, 17
Borno, Louis, 51
Bourbon dynasty, 17
bourgeoisie, Haitian, 57, 60n5, 69, 111n3; Duvalier, F., impacting, 51; landed, 11, 14, 48; mulatto and black factions struggling within, 73–74; wealth accumulated by, 34–35
Boyer, Jean-Pierre, 5, 10–11, 15, 37–38, 39n2; cronyism accused of, 31; indemnity agreed to by, 1, 6–7, 20–21; Ordinance of 17 April accepted by, 7–8, 21–22, 25; Pétion-Ville constructed by, 24; Praslin uprising against, 8, 16–17
Bwa Kale movement. *See* Sharp Stick movement

Cabon, Adolphe, 12–13
the Cacos (armed resistance), 46
Canada, 95, 99–101
Capital (Marx), 27
capitalism, 42, 65–68, 110
capitalist class, working class exploited by, 64–65, 68
capitalist firms, military power expanding, 41–42
Caracol Industrial Park, 81
CARDH. *See* Center for Analysis and Research on Human Rights
Caribbean, 44
Caribbean Community (CARICOM), 100

Las Casas, Barthelemy "baron de," 22, 24
Casimir, Jean, 28, 32
Castor, Suzy, 46, 49
Catholic Church, 53–54, 69, 87n3
Center for Analysis and Research on Human Rights (*Centre d'analyse et de recherche en droits de l'homme*) (CARDH), 93–94
Central America, 44
Centre d'analyse et de recherche en droits de l'homme. *See* Center for Analysis and Research on Human Rights
CEP. *See* Provisional Electoral Council
Chabrol, Comte de, 6, 39n3
Charles, Carolle, 63, 84–85
Charles X (king), 5, 11, 23
Chavez, Hugo, 90
Cheney, Paul, 28
Chérizier (gang leader), 95
children, Haitian, 77
chimères. *See* gangs
Christophe, Henri, 10, 14–15, 19–20
Cité Soleil (shantytown), in Port-au-Prince, 101–2
Clarkson, Thomas, 20
class, 64–65, 68, 71. *See also* middle class; ruling class; working class
class position, women impacted by, 63
Clermont-Tonnere (minister), 20
Clesca, Monique, 95, 101, 102
Clinton, Bill, 44, 55–56, 58
CNG. *See* Conseil National de Gouvernement
Coast Guard, U.S., 103
Code Rural (1826), 16
Collier, Paul, 58

INDEX

colonial property owners, expropriation of, 29–30, 39n9
color divisions, amongst Haitians, 18–19
"color line," 67
"color question," 43, 51
Columbus, Christopher, 27
Commission for Haitian Solution to the Crisis, 98
Congress of Verona, 7
Conseil Électoral Provisoire. See Provisional Electoral Council
Conseil National de Gouvernement (CNG), 53
constitution, U.S. imposing new, 47
Constitution of Haiti (1987), 72
Coradin, Jean, 7
Corredor, Elizabeth, 69
corruption, as prebend, 40n15
cronyism, Boyer accused of, 31
Cuba, 50

Dartiguenave, Sudre, 46
Dauxion-Lavaisse (emissary), 18–20
Debray, Régis, 8, 40n12
debt, double, 23–25
"Declaration of the People's Party on the Political Conjuncture of the Country" (*"Deklarasyon Pati Rasin Kan Pèp La Sou Konjonkti Politik Peyi A"*), 96–97
Del Rio, in Texas (U.S.), 103
democracy, maximalist, 55, 86
Department of Homeland Security (DHS), for U.S., 103
Dessalines, Jean-Jacques, 13–14, 31, 39n6, 97
development, assembly industry not generating, 81–82

development strategy, of Haiti, 50
DHS. *See* Department of Homeland Security
diesel fuel, shortage of, 90–91
discrimination, against women, 80
divisions of labor: gender, 61, 63, 78–79; slavery rationalized through, 66–67; social differences responding to, 63
domestic workers, wage laborers contrasted with, 70
Domingue, Michel, 35
Dominican Republic, 50, 77
double debt, 23–25, 31, 36
Draverman (emissary), 18
Dubois, W. E. B., 67
Dupetit-Thouars (envoy), 20
Duvalier, François, 2, 43, 51–52, 59n4, 107
Duvalier, Jean-Claude, 2, 43, 52–54, 81, 107

earthquake (2010), Haiti impacted by, 57–58, 81, 104, 107
Ebert, Teresa, 63, 69
economy, of Haiti: double debt and, 31; foreign capital dominating, 36–37; indemnity burdening, 30; lack of development of, 2
education, in Haiti, 75, 80
Ehrenreich, Barbara, 71
elections, in Haiti, 59nn3–4
elites, Haitian, 28
embezzlement, by officials, 39n6
emigrants, remittances from, 3, 74–75, 109
emigration crisis, from Haiti, 104–11
employers, unemployment advantaging, 75

employment, education and, 80
Engels, Frederick, 68, 70
England, independence not recognized by, 17–18
Esmangart (emissary), 20, 21
Espérance, Pierre, 96
Estimé, Dumarsais, 51
ethnicity, 67–68
Eugène, Itazienne, 29–30
Europe, 7
extractive industries, in Haiti, 50

Fanmi Lavalas. See Bald-Head Haitian Party
Farmer, Paul, 30
farmers, Haitian: landed peasant, 32–33, 47–48; tenant, 32–33; wage laborers transformed into by, 106
Fatton, Robert, 34, 50, 58, 98
feminist groups, 84–85
feminist movement, radical, 71–72
Ferron de la Ferronnays (plantation), 15
Fields, Barbara, 67
folklore, of Haiti, 112n6
Fontanges, François, 20
food insecurity, 76, 84
Foote, Daniel, 92, 103
Ford, Alessandro, 100
"Foreign Affairs" (Friedman), 41
foreign capital, 35–37
foreign debt, treasury compared with, 36
foreign investors: Haiti attracting, 81; heads of state borrowing from, 38–39; low-wage labor force sought by, 58–59. *See also* United States
former slaves, 31–32, 38
France, 5, 17; blockage threatened by, 22–23; color divisions exploiting, 18–19; Haiti attempted to be recontrolled by, 10–11, 20; independence recognized by, 1, 9, 22; military invasion not possible by, 20–21, 25; treaties signed between Haiti and, 23–24. *See also* indemnity
Fraser, Nancy, 71–72
free trade zones, in Haiti, 57, 81, 106
Frémont (colonel), 6
French Revolution, 40n11
Friedman, Thomas, 41–44

Gaillard, Roger, 47
gangs (*chimères*), 74, 91–93, 97–101; Haitian National Police suppressing, 96, 102; Port-au-Prince controlled by, 3, 93, 102; towns and communities controlled by, 96
Garcia, Marcus, 95
Gardella, Alexis, 72–73, 76
gasoline, shortage of, 90–91
GBV. *See* gender-based violence
Geffrard, Fabre-Nicolas, 35
gender: assembly industry and, 82–83; class and, 71; origin of ideology of, 66
gender-based violence (GBV), 93
gender divisions of labor, 61, 63, 78–79
gender roles, 87n3
Great Britain, 7
"growth with equity" model, 54
Guterres, Antonio, 100

Hagan, Tom, 101–2
Haiti. *See specific topics*
Haitian-American Agricultural Development Company, 49
Haitian American Sugar Company, 49

Haitian army, Haitian National Police, 97
Haitian government, IHRC displacing, 58
Haitian National Police, 100; Canada helping, 101; gangs suppressed by, 96, 102; Haitian army replaced by, 97
Haiti Economic Lift Program (HELP), 81, 107
Haïti en Marche, 111n4
"Haïti et la France" (*Rapport*) (report), 8, 40n12
Haiti Hemispheric Opportunity through Partnership Encouragement Act (HOPE), 81
Hall, Stuart, 62
Haut Conseil de Transition. *See* High Transitional Council
HCT. *See* High Transitional Council
heads of state, of Haiti, 38–39, 89–90, 97
HELP. *See* Haiti Economic Lift Program
Hemispheric Opportunity through Partnership Encouragement Act (HOPE), 107
Henry, Ariel, 3, 91–93, 98, 102; Biden supporting, 99–100; HTC formed by, 101; Montana Accord dismissed by, 99; UN addresses by, 104
high office, in Haiti, 72
High Transitional Council (*Haut Conseil de Transition*) (HCT), 101–3
Hispaniola, 25
HOPE. *See* Hemispheric Opportunity through Partnership Encouragement Act
households, Haitian, 75–76
Hyppolite, Florvil, 35

IFIs. *See* International Financial Institutions
IHRC. *See* Interim Haiti Reconstruction Commission
IMF. *See* International Monetary Fund
income, wealth differentiated from, 64, 87n1
income inequality, 56
indemnity, of Haiti to France, 36, 38; Aristide rejecting, 8; Bill of Impeachment not mentioning, 31; Boyer agreeing to, 1, 6–7, 20–21; economy burdened by, 30; history of negotiations since 1814 of, 10–11; independence and, 5, 23, 25–26; payment of, 29–30; Pétion offering, 19–20, 27–28; ruling class benefiting from, 29; unpopularity of, 30–31
independence, of Haiti: England not recognizing, 17–18; European countries recognizing, 24–25; France recognizing, 1, 9, 22; Great Britain not recognizing, 7; indemnity and, 5, 23, 25–26; U.S. not recognizing, 7, 17–18; war of, 13
inflation, Haiti impacted by, 108
Inginac, Joseph Baltazar, 6, 23
insecurity, food, 76, 84
Institute for Justice & Democracy in Haiti, 92, 94–95
Inter-American Development Bank, 57, 106
Interim Haiti Reconstruction Commission (IHRC), 58
International Financial Institutions (IFIs), 43, 52, 54, 56, 58, 81
international financial institutions, neoliberal policies imposed by, 2

International Halliwell Mines Limited, 49
International Monetary Fund (IMF), 55, 90, 111n4
investors, foreign. *See* foreign investors
Irish immigrants, in U.S., 67

Jaar, Rodolphe, 92–93
Janetsky, Megan, 76
Joachim, Benoit, 36
Joseph, Mario, 100
July Revolution, 23
Justice Department, for U.S., 92–93

Kenya, 100, 102–3

labor, Haitian, 12, 65; gender divisions of, 61, 63, 78–79; middle class selling, 69–70; unpaid domestic, 70; of women, 2–3. *See also* divisions of labor; slaves; wage laborers
labor force, 47–48
LaFeber, Walter, 44–45
landed bourgeoisie, 11, 14, 48
landed peasant farmers, 32–33, 47–48
Leclerc (general), 14
Léger, Abel-Nicolas, 8, 25, 31
Légitime, François, 35
Lescot, Élie, 51
Liberation Theology, 43, 54, 97–98
locked down (*lok*), 90
lok. *See* locked down
Louis Philippe (king), 23
Louis XVIII (king), 17, 21, 25
Louverture, Toussaint, 8, 11–13
low-wage labor force, 58–59, 82
Lundahl, Matts, 84
Luxemburg, Rosa, 69

MacDonald Company, U.S. intervening on behalf of, 46
Mackau, baron de, 6, 22, 39n3
Mackenzie, Charles, 24–25
Madiou, Thomas, 8, 21
Maduro, Nicolas, 90
Magloire, Paul, 49
Malouet, Pierre-Victor, 10, 17–18
manba. *See* peanut butter
mangoes, 78, 79
Marines, U.S., 44, 46, 55–56
Marius, Philippe-Richard, 73
Mars, Louis-Henri, 102
Martelly, Michel, 89, 95, 98, 111n2
Marx, Karl, 27, 33, 75, 82–84
maximalist democracy, 55, 86
Medina, Franco de, 18–19, 39n8
Meiksins, Ellen, 55
men, Haitian, 61, 68–69
métayage (farming system), 77–78
Michel, Andrée, 62
middle class, Haitian: labor sold by, 69–70; mulatto and black factions struggling within, 73–74; in urban areas, 50
migrants, Haitian, 103
military power, capitalist firms expanded by, 41–42
minimum wage, 82, 109
Ministry on the Status and Rights of Women, 85
MINUSTAH. *See* United Nations Mission to Haiti
Moïse, Claude, 46, 53, 108
Moïse, Jovenel, 3, 82, 92, 98; assassination of, 74, 89; opposition to, 90–91; U.S. voted with by, 91
Mollien (consul), 24

INDEX

157

Montana Accord, 98–99, 101, 103

National Assembly (1789), 40n11
National Convention (1794), 40n11
neoliberal policies, 2, 53, 58, 81, 107
The New York Times (newspaper), 9, 41–42, 92
Nixon, Richard, 52
North, Oliver, 54

occupation, by U.S., 44, 105, 111; balance of power transformed by, 50; objectives of, 43; Wilson justifying, 45
Office of the High Commissioner for Human Rights, 93
officials, embezzlement by, 39n6
Okin, Susan Moller, 71
Olivier, Émile, 53
Ordinance of 17 April (1825), 7–8, 21–22, 25, 28, 38
Orélien, Garry, 92
Organization of American States, 91
Osias, Gracita, 83
Other Worlds report, 83

Paris Treaty (May 1814), 17
patriarchy, transition to, 68
patronage, system of, 72–73
Péan, Leslie, 30, 36
peanut butter (*manba*), 78–79
peanuts, 78
peasant farmers, landed, 32–33, 47–48
peasants, Haitian, 50, 74, 83, 106
Pesce, Fernanda, 76
Pétion, Alexandre, 2, 10, 14, 37–38, 39n2, 39n7; indemnity offered by, 19–20, 27–28; plantations under, 15–16; quid pro quo introduced by, 1
Pétion-Ville, in Haiti, 24, 89
Petrocaribe fund, 90
Philippe, Louis, 28
Phillips, Anthony, 30
Pierre, Alfred, 109
Pierre, Guy, 50
Pierre-Charles, Gérard, 36
Piketty, Thomas, 110
plantations, 31; Christophe revitalizing, 15; disappearance of, 32; Louverture militarizing, 12–13; under Pétion, 15–16; revolutionary government maintaining, 11
police. *See* Haitian National Police
Pons, Moya, 16
Port-au-Prince, in Haiti, 3, 30, 76, 92–93, 102
Porter, Catherine, 30
Portes, Alejandro, 105
poverty, in Haiti, 59
Praslin uprising, 8, 16–17, 39n4
prebend, corruption as, 40n15
presidents, Haitian, 59n3
Préval, René, 57, 90
property: elites transferred, 28; nationalization of, 14; question of, 17–29; revolutionary government redistributing, 12; sacred principle of, 26–27; social order based on, 26
Provisional Electoral Council (*Conseil Électoral Provisoire*) (CEP), 101

race, 62, 66–68
racism, 67
radical feminist movement, 71–72
"The Ransom" (reports), 9

Rapport. See "Haïti et la France"
Rasanbleman Sosyalis pou yon Inisyativ Nasyonal tou Nèf. See Assembly of the People's Socialist Party for a New National Initiative
remittances, from emigrants, 3, 74–75, 109
restavèk. See stay/live with
Rethinking the Haitian Revolution, 1
revolutionary government, in Haiti, 11–12
Reynolds Mining Corporation, 49
rice, from U.S., Haiti importing, 56
Richelieu, Duc de, 21
Rigaud, André, 39n7
Rochambeau (general), 14
Roediger, David, 67
Rouanez (senator), 6
ruling class, Haitian: foreign capital exploiting, 35; former slaves not expropriated by, 38; indemnity benefited from by, 29; in rural areas, 73–74; in urban areas, 73–74. *See also* bourgeoisie
rural areas, in Haiti, 73–74, 77, 83

Sae-A Trading Co., 108
Saget, Nissage, 35
Saint-Dic, Jacques Ted, 101
Saint-Domingue, 5, 17, 111
Saint-Macary (envoy), 23
Salnave, Sylvain, 35
Salomon, Lysius, 24, 35
Sam, T. Antoine, 36
Sam, Vilbrun Guillaume, 45
Santo Domingo, 11, 16, 30
Schneider, Mark, 101
Schoelcher, Victor, 8, 11

Sea-A Trading Co., Ltd., 81
sexual violence, against women, 75–76
sharecroppers, 32–33, 40n14, 48, 77–78
Sharp Stick movement (*Bwa Kale* movement), 93–94
Single Health Information System, 93
slave labor, 59n2
slavery, 66–67, 77
slaves, Haitian: former, 31–32, 38; of Saint-Domingue, 111; wage laborers distinguished from, 87n2
Smith, Adam, 42
SMP. *See* Staff-Monitored Program
social mobility, 51
Solidarity Among Haitian Women (SOFA), 85
Soulouque, Faustin, 97
South Americans, U.S. migrated to by, 103–4
the Spanish, Taino population killed by, 26
Staff-Monitored Program (SMP), by IMF, 111n4
stay/live with (*restavèk*), 76–77

Taino population, the Spanish killing, 26
Temporary Protected Status (TPS), for Haiti, 103
tenant farmers, sharecroppers distinguished from, 32–33
Tèt Kalé (political party), 91
Texas (U.S.), 103
Tontons Macoutes. See Volunteers of National Security
Toussaint, Eddy, 30
TPS. *See* Temporary Protected Status
trade sector, 80
treasury, of Haiti, 36, 72–73

Trouillot, Michel-Rolph, 52
Trudeau, Justin, 95, 99–100
Trujillo government, 50
Trump, Donald, 91
Türk, Volker, 99–100
Turnier, Alain, 31, 38–39

UN. *See* United Nations
unemployment, in Haiti, 83; assembly industry not solving, 82, 108; employers advantaged by, 75; rate of, 60n6; in urban areas, 79–80
United Nations (UN), 99–100, 102–4
United Nations Mission to Haiti (MINUSTAH), 57, 100–101
United States (U.S.), 2, 41, 52–54, 98, 101; Coast Guard of, 103; constitution imposed by, 47; DHS for, 103; independence not recognized by, 7, 17–18; Irish immigrants in, 67; Justice Department for, 92–93; MacDonald Company intervened on behalf of by, 46; Moïse, J., voting with, 91; rice imported to Haiti from, 56; sanctions imposed by, 95; South Americans migrating to, 103–4; Texas in, 103. *See also* occupation, by U.S.
unpaid domestic labor, 70
urban areas, of Haiti: middle class in, 50; ruling class in, 73–74; unemployment in, 79–80; working class in, 83
U.S. *See* United States
U.S. Agency for International Development (USAID), 106

Vendryes, B., 26–27, 40n11

Vincent, Sténio, 45, 51
violence, gender-based, 75–76, 93
Volunteers of National Security (*Tontons Macoutes*), 51, 97

wage laborers: domestic workers contrasted with, 70; farmers transforming into, 106; slaves distinguished from, 87n2
wage-labor force, 48–49
Walton, John, 105
wealth, 34–35, 64, 87n1
Wealth of Nations, 42
Weber, Max, 40n15
Wilson, Woodrow, 45
women, Haitian, 68; androcentric norms devaluing, 70–71; class position impacting, 63; discrimination against, 80; education of, 75; exploitation of poor, 83; in high office, 72; households headed by, 76; labor of, 2–3; mangoes sold by, 78; men enriched by, 61; peanuts sold by, 78; in rural areas, 83; sexual violence against, 75–76; of working class, 69
women's groups, demands of, 86
women's organizations, 84–85
workers, proletarianization of, 43, 49
working class, Haitian, 74; capitalist class exploiting, 64–65, 68; in urban areas, 83; women of, 69. *See also* farmers; wage laborers
World Bank, 52, 74, 80–81, 106
World War II, 8
Wucker, Michelle, 11

Zinglins (terror squad), 97

About the Author

Alex Dupuy is John E. Andrus Professor of Sociology, Emeritus at Wesleyan University in Middletown, Connecticut. At Wesleyan he served as chair of the Sociology Department and the African American Studies Department and as dean of the Social Sciences. He is an internationally recognized scholar and specialist on Haiti. In 2017 he received the Haitian Studies Association Lifetime Achievement Award in Recognition of a lifetime of exceptional scholarship and outstanding contribution to Haitian Studies. He has lectured at universities and colleges across the United States and abroad and has given many interviews and commentaries on Haitian affairs on local, national, and international radio and television networks and local, national, and international newspapers, including *The New York Times*, *The Washington Post*, *The Guardian*, the *PBS News Hour*, Toronto Public TV, Democracy Now!, WBAI, National Public Radio, Pacifica Radio, the BBC, the CBC, Radio France International, BBC World News, and the Australian Broadcasting Company. In addition to his many articles in professional journals and anthologies, he is the author of *Haiti in the World Economy: Class, Race, and Underdevelopment Since 1700* (1989); *Haiti in the New World Order: The Limits of the Democratic Revolution* (1997); *The Prophet and Power: Jean-Bertrand Aristide, the International Community, and Haiti* (2007); *Haiti: From Revolutionary Slaves to Powerless Citizens: Essays on the Politics and Economics of Underdevelopment (1804–2013)* (2014); and *Rethinking the Haitian Revolution: Slavery, Independence, and the Struggle for Recognition* (2019).

www.ingramcontent.com/pod-product-compliance
Lightning Source LLC
Chambersburg PA
CBHW030656230426
43665CB00011B/1120